DIVORCE

Divorce as a Catalyst for an
Ext

D E B B I E   F O R D

HarperSanFrancisco
A Division of HarperCollinsPublishers

Also by Debbie Ford

The Dark Side of the Light Chasers
The Right Questions
The Best Year of Your Life

Library of Congress Cataloging-in-Publication Data is available.
ISBN-13: 978–0–06–122712–7
ISBN-10: 0–06–122712–9

07 08 09 10   RRD(H)   10 9 8 7 6 5

To all the children in the world

who have suffered the pain of divorce,

and

to my son, Beau,

for being the light of my life.

CONTENTS

CONTENTS

FOREWORD

Anger, fear, heartache, guilt, helplessness, sadness, loss, relief, and powerlessness are just a few of the emotions that might be running through your body at this moment. Thoughts like, How can I get through this? Will this ever end? Why is this happening to me? I can't make it on my own. I should have left earlier. I'll never be happy again. These are the bitter, obsessive fragments of mind chatter that might be running through your head, disturbing your sleep, robbing you of your joy, interfering with your ability to be present for your family or your work, and devouring countless hours of your life.

Does this sound familiar? This is the process of divorce, of separating from someone you love or once loved. It is a horribly lonely time, with the emptiness of loss tugging on every choice and encroaching on your ability to think clearly. This is a time when you will more than likely question who you are, where you have been, who you loved, and the choices you made or didn't make. This is the time when you will examine your worth, assess your values and, hopefully, decide that you deserve to heal your heart and move on with your life. I use the words "heal your heart" with some hesitancy, because the truth is that our hearts our already healed. They cannot be broken. Underneath the deep pain and the dark feelings that obscure the love that is alive inside of us, our hearts are perfectly intact. They are, even if masked by disorienting sadness, filled with love, peace and contentment.

So what is it that gets in the way so that we can't feel the good stuff and are left only with the bad? Why do we experience heartache and hopelessness and feelings of despair? This is how it works: think of the sun for a moment and its bright shining rays that warm the earth and send energy to the fields so that our crops can grow. It is always perfect. It always knows what to do and when to do it. But often we cannot see the sun because it is hidden behind a cloud. Maybe there will be rays of sunlight breaking through from time to time, but other times it will appear as if the sun does not exist. But we know this is not true; it has been proven that the sun is there even in the midst of a destructive hurricane or a blinding blizzard. The same is true about our heart. It is always there with the power to illuminate our lives and nurture a new future. It is always there with the power to bring us healthy love, emotional healing, hope, and possibility, and, most importantly, peace of mind. Our hearts and the good feelings that exist within and around them are just beneath the emotional cloud cover, waiting for the storm to pass.

Heartache and emotional pain are merely clouds—an accumulation of negative emotions. Yes, they might be black clouds, clouds like you've never experienced before in your life, but still, they are only clouds. *Spiritual Divorce* and the process that is offered in the pages that follow are designed to support you in dissolving those clouds so you can create a life of deep meaning—a life that you love.

You deserve to heal completely from whatever you are going through. No matter what you have done, what mistakes you've made, or where you are at this moment, the possibility for a life beyond what you can imagine awaits you right now. The process will not always be easy, but if you allow it, it will be profound and life-changing. It will be a time for you to grow and evolve and open up to parts of yourself that you have never encountered. It will be a time to step into a new evolution of yourself and look at who you are and how you can live life in an entirely different manner.

It has been six and a half years since the conception of *Spiritual Divorce* I am writing this new introduction because every time I lead a seminar or give a lecture several people always come up to me just to thank me for this book. The same message in different words comes out of their mouths: "*Spiritual Divorce* saved my life. At a time when I thought I was drowning, I learned to swim. Thank you."

I give deep thanks to the one I call God, because writing this book was truly a divine experience. There was never a moment when I didn't feel guided and compelled to share my pain and heartache, as well as my joys and triumphs. Even after I wrote this book I had an opportunity to read it again and use it myself to get through another failed relationship. Once again I was able to see that these principles that I wrote about are imperative for good mental health. They are vital if we want to learn from our past, grow and evolve, and most importantly, if we want to leave the past where it belongs—in the past. Then we are free to move on to greater realities and deeper loves.

I invite you to enter fully into this spiritual experience, the experience of lifting the cloud cover that hides your ever-loving heart.

Debbie Ford

A HOLY MOMENT

A life unexamined is not worth living.

SOCRATES

By the end of our first year of marriage I think we both knew it would never last. I lived in my world, and Dan lived in his. Many times we tried to come together and heal our relationship, but there was always a block on either Dan's side or mine. Then one day I asked Dan to sit down so we could discuss our problems. Moments later all of Dan's withheld emotions, which had been pent up since the time I was pregnant, were released. I sat there, stunned, as I listened to all of my husband's anger, resentment, and dissatisfaction. Dan finally expressed his truth, and a few weeks later he moved out.

I felt as if I was caught in the middle of the second act of a bad play. The third act was about to begin, and the outcome could go either way. I could choose to be relieved and call my marriage quits, or I could hold on to the dream of living happily ever after, until death do us part. Now I was torn between two worlds, and neither one held the promise of happiness.

I had waited thirty-eight years to find the right person to share my life with me. I had promised myself that I would never do to my children what my parents had done to me. I was thirteen when my mother broke the devastating news to my sister, brother, and me that my father had moved out and their marriage was over. My father's departure from the house started the painful process of learning to live without "a real family." It took me more than ten years of therapy and too many tears to count to come to terms with the pain of my parents' divorce. I promised myself that my children would grow up in a happy home with both a mother and a father who loved them. It shook every bone in my body to think that now I too was going to fail, and that my son would be a product of "a broken home."

As I faced my shattered reality, my emotions changed as often as the weather outside. One moment I was calm and hopeful; the next I was depressed and withdrawn. There wasn't anything I didn't blame Dan for, and I was sure the collapse of our marriage was entirely his fault. I didn't understand why Dan couldn't change and be the man I thought I had married. In the wake of my pain I asked myself, *Why is this happening? Why can't I stop it? And why am I reliving my worst nightmare?*

It was asking these questions that seemed to have no answers that led me to the process of creating a Spiritual Divorce. These questions forced me to look deep within myself and to examine my inner world. Many sleepless nights I lay in bed trying to figure out what had gone wrong and how I had managed to create so much anger and resentment in my partner when my deepest desire was to have a happy marriage. How could I have been so blind? What had kept me from seeing the signs of distress that now seemed so clear?

Somehow I knew that if I didn't find and heal the parts of myself that had kept me from having a loving, nurturing relationship, I would be doomed to living a life without a loving partner. As the days passed, it became increasingly obvious that I could either use this time to beat myself up or I could choose to see my divorce as a spiritual process, a journey toward wholeness. It was an opportunity to observe, question, and transform behaviors that no longer served me. Deep down I knew I had only one choice—to use my divorce as a catalyst for building a new foundation for my life. Learning about myself, examining my beliefs, and dissecting my judgments became the center of my focus.

SPIRITUAL WAKE-UP CALLS

Life presents us with many opportunities to awaken to our divine nature, the highest expression of ourselves. Some people call these opportunities spiritual wake-up calls. Most of the time they appear during times of great distress. Divorce is one of these times. It is during this crisis that we have the opportunity to explore our inner world and begin the process of becoming intimate with our entire self, our light as well as our darkness.

Pain is a great motivator that breaks down the walls that keep old behaviors intact. Pain guides us toward thoughts and ideas that we might otherwise push away, and it forces us to seek answers from places we've never looked before. Pain opens our minds to ideas that hold the key to new insight, understanding, and freedom. Emotional turmoil can be a powerful catalyst to reconnect us with our divine nature. It propels us into a journey of self-discovery and urges us to learn how to love and accept our entire being. Healing our emotional turmoil delivers us freedom from pain and prevents us from repeating the patterns of our past.

It's been said that you will learn more in ten days of agony than in ten years of contentment. Pain can be your greatest teacher—a friend telling you what parts of your life need attention. Sri Swami Satchidananda, founder of the worldwide Integral Yoga Institutes, explains pain as a wake-up call. He asks you to imagine being sound asleep when you are suddenly awakened by the fire alarm in your bedroom. Startled, you jump out of bed, run to the closet, and take out a baseball bat. You smash the alarm into smithereens until it stops ringing. But then, instead of looking for the fire, you put the bat back in the closet, crawl back into bed, and go to sleep.

Pain is an alarm, a warning, signaling to us that there is something burning. If we want to live happy, contented lives, we need to stay awake and tend to the flames that prevent us from basking in a well of inner peace. Pain is a signal that an emotional fire rages close by, that something within us needs care and healing. If we tend to our pain, we will be guided back to a place of peace and tranquillity. Pain is a sacred emotion that allows us to discover who we really are. It leads us to places we would never go on our own.

This is a time when you need to be completely and radically honest, because honesty is the only way to step out of pain and suffering. As long as we continue to deny our truth and our partner's truth, we will continue to live in isolated pain. As humans, we are masters at rationalizing behaviors, justifying deceit, and manipulating facts in order to make ourselves feel better. But no matter what stories we tell ourselves, or how we blame others or justify our positions, at some level we always know the truth. Remember the adage: "The truth will set you free." By being willing to look at the stories we've told ourselves, we allow ourselves to begin the process of transformation.

It might just be that learning to love the totality of ourselves—the "good" and the "not-so-good"—is the most difficult task to which we're ever assigned. We've been taught that in order to feel loved, we need to find someone to love us. But when that love fails, it's not surprising that we fall back into whatever negative programming we've been carrying around about love and life to explain the failure to ourselves. Fear, frustration, sadness, and loneliness may become our constant companions. Thoughts that we are unlovable or undesirable add to our feelings of worthlessness as we struggle for answers to the "why" of our situations.

Often we become depressed or angry and have inner dialogues like "I can't trust anyone," "life sucks," or "I'll never let anyone do that to me again." All of our negative feelings and painful messages are stuffed within our consciousness. Left unexamined, we turn these toxic emotions and negative beliefs back on ourselves. Neglecting our inner wounds results in abusive relationships, addictions, obsessions, depressions, chronic illness, and a negative view of ourselves, others, and the world. And to make things worse, if we don't take the opportunity to look at ourselves and heal our pain, we are likely to repeat our failures.

It's imperative that we use this time to heal. Healing is the primary path returning us to a place where we see the perfection of our humanity. It is this awareness that gives us the opportunity to return to the deepest connection available to anyone—our connection with our Divine Creator.

A SPIRITUAL DIVORCE

A Spiritual Divorce is one in which we use our divorce to improve our lives and our experience becomes one of gain rather than loss. A Spiritual Divorce brings us back into the presence of our highest self and heals the split between our ego and our soul. When we use our divorces to heal our wounds, to learn, grow, and develop ourselves into more loving, conscious human beings, we have truly had a spiritual experience and a liberation of our souls. Rather than staying stuck in the pain of our broken hearts, a Spiritual Divorce calls us to reconnect to the highest aspects of our being. It is here in the presence of our highest self that we can reclaim our power, our joy, and the limitless freedom to create the life of our dreams.

If you're going through a divorce right now, this may sound like a tall order, an impossible task. You may be having the worst experience of your life and can't even consider the possibility that your divorce could turn into something positive. Or you may be relieved to call it quits. Pain and change are the keys that open the door to a deeper understanding of our human experience. The pain of divorce breaks down our defenses, leaving us in a place of complete vulnerability. And it is only in this place of complete vulnerability that we become quiet enough to experience the greater realities of peace and contentment.

THE SEVEN SPIRITUAL LAWS OF DIVORCE

It is important to know that the breakdown of your relationship is for a greater purpose. Understanding some of the basic spiritual laws of the Universe will help you to discover that there is a reason you're going through this pain. These laws will guide you through the process of healing and bring you back to a place deep inside that is filled with wisdom, knowledge, and compassion for the human experience.

1. The Law of Acceptance: The first and possibly the most important spiritual law is that *everything is as it should be.* Nothing occurs by accident, and there are no coincidences. We are always evolving, whether we are aware of it or not. And our lives are divinely designed for each one of us to get exactly what we need to support our own unique evolutionary process.

2. The Law of Surrender: *When we stop resisting and surrender to the situation exactly as it is, things begin to change.* Resistance is the number-one culprit in denying us our right to heal. We resist out of fear that if we let go, if we surrender, our lives will go out of control or we will be faced with circumstances that we can't handle. When we are willing to look at our situation and admit that we don't know how to fix it, we are ready to get the help we need.

3. The Law of Divine Guidance: *God will do for you what you cannot do for yourself.* When you get out of your own way and let go of your defenses, you become humble. Humility is the doorway through which the Divine can walk into your life. Without humility, we believe we can do it ourselves. Without humility, our false sense of pride, or ego, prohibits us from seeing the entire situation with clear eyes. Our egos remain in charge until we step outside our righteous belief that we are

independent and separate beings. As long as this myth is intact, we keep the door closed to our higher wisdom.

4. The Law of Responsibility: *With divine guidance, we can look at exactly how we participated in and co-created our divorce drama.* We can begin to take responsibility for our entire situation and make peace with our past. We can see how we have chosen the perfect partner to teach us the perfect lessons. Once we have asked God to come into our lives and guide us, we begin to heal.

5. The Law of Choice: *Having taken responsibility, we can choose new interpretations that empower us.* We become responsible and the designer of our own new reality. We can separate from our partner and cut the karmic cords by taking back the aspects of ourselves that we've projected onto our mate. We can distinguish what our self-defeating behaviors have been and learn how to act instead of react in difficult situations.

6. The Law of Forgiveness: *After we have cut the karmic cord, we will be able to ask God to forgive us.* Asking for forgiveness allows us to let go of our judgments and beliefs about what is right and what is wrong and find compassion for our entire self. Compassion unfolds when we are in the presence of the perfection of the Universe, when we can experience ourselves in another. It comes with the great understanding of the difficulties and ambiguity of being a human being. Compassion is God's grace for those who ask. Once we have received compassion for ourselves, we will be able to find compassion and forgiveness for our mate.

7. The Law of Creation: *Experiencing the freedom of forgiveness opens up the gates to new realities.* Forgiveness breaks all the cords that keep us tied to the past. It allows us to experience an innocent heart filled with love and excitement for life.

This is the time to create a new future, one grounded in your divine truth.

These seven spiritual laws are a guide and will serve as a reference point for your healing process. This book will take you through the steps of understanding, practicing, and integrating these basic spiritual principles. They are designed to help you break through your fears, dissolve your pain, and understand the deeper meaning of your situation. When these laws are integrated and practiced they will give you the freedom to create the life you have always dreamed of.

Free will enables us to choose the direction in which we will take our lives. To choose a Spiritual Divorce is to choose to use your divorce to heal yourself. You can choose to work hard and heal yourself on the deepest level, or you can choose to be a victim of life and other people's problems. In other words, you can choose to *use* your divorce, or you can let your divorce *use* you. Until you seek to find and embrace the gift of any situation or problem, it continues to use you. It holds you prisoner, and you carry it around as an open wound wherever you go.

KARMIC CORDS

Our emotional wounds unwittingly echo the pain of our past and act as guides leading us to those places within ourselves that need healing. These wounds cause us to resonate with people who have similar or matching unhealed emotional issues. Attaching us to these people are energetic connectors I think of as karmic cords. There is a sense of destiny at work here: these karmic cords—cords of fate—bring people into our lives who are tailor-made to bring us the spiritual experiences we need to complete ourselves.

These cords act like radio waves, calling forth all the experiences from the outer world that we need to heal our inner wounds. Until we receive the information and the lessons that are encoded in these wounds, we will stay stuck. Karmic relationships are here for us to learn, grow, and evolve into the highest manifestation of our own potential. Our souls know who we are at our highest level, and even though at the level of our conscious self we may not understand why something is happening, our soul is keenly aware of the experiences we need.

Even if you have been wronged, screwed, deceived, or mistreated, no situation you encounter in your life is accidental. Each situation is there to move you to the next level of awareness. Your job is to figure out how this is true and to discover the contribution that each event can make in your life. There are many steps to take to arrive at this truth. This book will support you through all the stages necessary to arrive at a place of deep healing and gratitude for your life.

We grow and heal when we take every event and find its blessing. Then we're able to use our experience to contribute to others and ourselves. If you believe, as I do, that there are no accidents and that everything happens as it should, then you can assume that the breakdown of your marriage is ultimately for your highest good. Let me repeat this: *the breakdown of your marriage is for your highest good.* I know that right now this concept may seem overwhelming, and it may even make you angry. But I promise you that as soon as you look at your life from this perspective, things will begin to change. It is a huge shift to understand that life is your teacher and that in every instance the Universe is guiding you toward the fulfillment of your highest self.

Once you've had the experience of being blessed by your divorce, your open wounds will begin to heal and your closed heart will begin to open. Transformation is the natural evolution of finding the gift of a negative experience, seeing the light in the darkness. Once you've discovered this valuable lesson, the excitement of life begins to filter in again. Then real magic happens when you begin opening up to new worlds, seeing opportunities you haven't been able to see before. Divorce becomes a holy moment when you choose to use it as a catalyst for having an extraordinary life.

This book is about having a spiritual awakening, a transformation, a reuniting of your heart and soul. Whether you are suffering from a broken heart or broken dreams, this process will allow you to see your life through the eyes of God.

HEALING ACTION STEPS

1. Select a journal that you love and dedicate it to the sole purpose of helping you to heal and grow through your divorce. Use it freely and frequently to express whatever feelings, thoughts, or insights arise within you. Keep your journal nearby to use during these exercises.

2. Take a few slow, deep breaths, allowing your body and mind to relax completely. Dedicate this time to furthering your healing and promoting your well-being. Close your eyes and allow your attention to rest in the area of your heart. Now imagine what it would be like to use your divorce as a spiritual journey. Consider for a moment that the feelings and circumstances surrounding this event are here to awaken you. Declare that the process you are going through right now is a holy one, divinely designed to bring about a positive change in your life. As you do this exercise, you may find that what arises in you is anger, upset, or resistance to acknowledging your divorce as a spiritual journey. Trust that whatever emerges is perfect and appropriate. When you are ready, slowly open your eyes and free-write your feelings, thoughts, or insights in your journal.

THE LAW OF

ACCEPTANCE

Chapter One

THINGS AREN'T
ALWAYS WHAT
THEY SEEM

In the depths of winter, I finally learned that within me
there lay an invincible summer.

ALBERT CAMUS, *SUMMER* (1954)

D ivine guidance lays the foundation that gives us the support and understanding we need to begin practicing the Law of Acceptance. Acceptance is the essential ingredient that enables us to begin the healing process. We cannot accept a situation until we're ready to look fearlessly at the facts of our circumstances. We can't heal what we cannot see, and we can't heal what we cannot feel. Yet too often the pain from our past and our fears of the future keep us stuck and unable to see our lives as a whole. Our blurred vision prohibits us from being in the present and opening up to higher levels of awareness. "It is only when we have the courage to face things exactly as they are, without any self-deception or illusion," the *I Ching* states, "that a light will develop out of events, by which the path to success may be recognized."

Acceptance comes when we step out of denial and judgment and are willing to see the present exactly as it exists in this moment, without any drama or story line. Drama keeps us stuck in an endless spiral of excuses that prevent us from being able to distinguish between fact and fantasy. Our drama serves as a defense mechanism designed to protect us from the pain of our past. When we're caught up in our drama, we are no longer living in the present moment. Instead, we get hooked into every similar experience from our past that was left unhealed. We think we are responding to the challenges of our lives when in fact we are reacting to all of our unresolved pain.

We must realize that what is happening in this moment is calling us to heal what happened to us in the past. To break free from the confines of our story we must distinguish what is real from what is unreal. What is from the past and what is happening now? What is our present-day pain and what is the unresolved pain of our past?

The drama of our story blinds us from seeing clearly the facts of our lives. Our drama is always personal. Its theme is "something is happening to me." Our story can always be traced back to some underlying issue that's been with us since childhood. For example: "I'm not lovable," "I can't trust men," "People aren't there for me when I need them," "Love doesn't last." Our story is invariably laced with "life is doing it to me."

An important aspect of our healing is learning how to separate the facts from the story. Fact is an unbiased observation of the events of our lives. Fiction is the story we create out of our unresolved emotions from the past. It is rarely based on the facts. Here are some examples that can help you to differentiate between fact and fiction:

> "My wife left me" (fact) versus "My wife left because I am unworthy of love" (fiction)

> "My husband emptied out our checking account" (fact) versus "My husband has deceived me and ruined my life forever" (fiction)

> "My child had an emotional episode at school " (fact) versus "My child has been damaged for life by my separation" (fiction)

Distinguishing the facts of our lives from the fiction lays the foundation for acceptance.

When Dan and I separated, I was filled with fear and became overly dramatic. I was sure that my life was over and that my son would suffer from the same emotional problems I had experienced as a child of divorced parents. After weeks of torturing myself, I decided to write down exactly what was going on in my life without all the dramatic side effects. My list looked like this:

1. I don't have any money of my own put away.

2. My husband doesn't want to continue going to therapy.

3. He doesn't see any reason to get a divorce, even though we aren't living together.

4. I will have to live inside his budget until I find a job.

5. I will have to get a job.

6. Dan will take my son for sixteen hours a week.

7. We will sell our house.

8. I will rent a home for my son and myself.

9. I will no longer cook dinner every night for Dan.

10. We will no longer be a couple.

11. I will have to pay my own bills.

After looking at the list, all of the internal noise that amounted to a lot of drama about Dan not loving me, or how I failed at yet another relationship, disappeared. In light of the facts of the situation, my exaggerated fear that I'd be living on the street seemed silly. Every upsetting thought I had about Dan taking Beau away from me vanished. Inside my mind I had been having hundreds of crazy thoughts that contributed to a belief that my life was ending. Distinguishing between fact and fiction became liberating. The facts demonstrated that only my marriage was ending, not my life. And the facts showed that I was going to have to make some changes. Even though I didn't welcome these changes initially, by writing them down I realized I could handle them all.

Distinguishing between my story and the facts was a life-changing experience. It afforded me the freedom to view the events of my life apart from the dramatic hell I was living in. "Divine detachment is when the lower self steps away from the drama it has created and allows the higher self to observe and comment upon it, clearly and without emotion; honestly and without hesitation; completely and without reservation," explains Neale Donald Walsh, author of the *Conversations with God* series. He goes on to say: "You will know when this process is working for you because there will be no negativity, no judgment, no anger, no shame, no guilt, no fear, no recrimination or sense of being made wrong—just a simple statement of what is so. And that statement may be very illuminating."

Living in the story of our divorce and the drama of our circumstances comes with a huge emotional price. It costs us peace of mind and prevents us from living in the present. It denies us access to the clarity of our wisest self and keeps us stuck in the pain of our past. Most of us don't realize all the ways we use our story to make ourselves feel important or to get attention. Recognizing our need to dramatize divorce helps us to break the unconscious motivation that prevents us from seeing with clear, loving eyes.

Divorce often causes us to look at the other dramas we've created. Linda had been married to Warren for nine years before having a beautiful baby boy, Zachary. Although Warren had been combating a horrible illness for several years, when their son arrived, Linda felt that their life together would now be complete. Linda always lived with the fantasy that one day she would have a real family, and now it seemed that dream was coming true—she had her husband and now a child of their very own. Then one day, when Zachary was only three months old, Warren told Linda that the stress of living with her was too much for him to be able to recover from his illness. Shortly thereafter he moved out.

Linda was emotionally unstable and had been abusing prescription drugs. Her story was that she needed these drugs to cope with Warren's illness. When Warren left her, she crashed into a deep depression, convinced that she had no reason for living. Linda be-lieved that she was nothing without Warren and had no purpose or value to anyone—especially her son. Now that Warren had fled from her fantasy life, she had to accept that she desperately needed help.

Warren supported Linda in getting the help she needed. She had never had friends and was frightened of everything. Despite the fact that she was an attractive, intelligent, and gentle woman, she saw no good in herself. She lived her life inside of the story that she had nothing to offer the world. So when Warren found a girlfriend, Linda saw this as God's way of taking care of Zachary, because she believed that she couldn't take care of him herself. From inside of her story that she "would never be a good mother," this was the only way she could see Warren's new relationship. Linda's own painful childhood had left her paralyzed with fear that she would be a terrible mother like her own. Yet Linda longed to be a good mother to her son more than any-thing in the world.

Warren's departure was the darkest moment of Linda's life, and it sent her into a spiral that caused her to hit bottom. Shattered and broken, she got off drugs and accepted help for the first time in her life. Her dark moment turned into a blessing in disguise. Because of Warren's absence, Linda started attending meetings, going to therapy, reading books, making real friends, and becoming the mother she al-ways wanted to be.

What Linda discovered was that her feelings were important and she needed to feel all of them in order to heal. She also discovered that *having* her feelings didn't mean that she *was* her feelings. And she learned that her overindulgence with her feelings fed the drama of her life and her divorce. Linda discovered how to distinguish between fic-tion and fact in order to break free from the emotional turbulence of her self-created drama. Now Linda took a look at her beliefs about herself to discover what was fact and what was fiction. She had noth-ing to offer (fiction) versus she had never had a job (fact). She couldn't have a family life without Warren (fiction) versus she and Zachary were a beautiful family (fact). She had no value without Warren (fiction) versus she was invaluable as the mother of Zachary and a member of society (fact). She was unworthy and unlovable (fiction) versus at certain times of the day she experienced feelings of unworthiness and unlovability (fact). She needed drugs to cope (fiction) versus she needed to learn coping skills and how to be self-nurturing (fact).

Although Linda had never had a job or kept a schedule, through her recovery she was able to work as a teacher's assistant for her son's kindergarten class. To her own surprise, she got up early and was able to get herself and Zachary ready and to school on time. During this period Linda also discovered how good she was with kids. With Linda at his side, Zachary became the star pupil in his class, and Linda found herself, one day at a time, becoming happier and more self-confident. She recognized that the great drama surrounding her life had been created by all of her false beliefs. Denial had disguised the real issues. The turning point came when she triumphantly accepted the fact that she had the power to change her life. Until she distinguished the facts from her stories, Linda was unable to accept her situation.

Practicing acceptance, of even the worst circumstances, is a powerful, life-changing tool. Even addicts and alcoholics whose situations seem dire are urged in their recovery to deal with life on the terms it presents. The *Big Book* of Alcoholics Anonymous offers us this assertion: "Acceptance is the answer to all my problems today. When I am disturbed, it is because I find some person, place or thing, or situation—some fact of my life—unacceptable to me, and I can find no serenity until I accept that person, place, thing or situation as being exactly the way it is supposed to be at this moment." Remembering these words of wisdom can shift a moment of suffering into a moment of peace. Without the faith that life is just as it should be, we cannot accept people, places, and things as they are. We will always be trying to change, manipulate, and control the outer world. Resisting your own truth, and the truth of other people's behavior, only takes you further into the darkness of denial.

THE TRANCE OF DENIAL

Denial is a defense mechanism of the ego that puts blinders over our eyes and plugs in our ears so that we're unable to experience life as it truly is—*without the story.* Denial kills off all other realities because when we are stuck in the trance of denial, we believe that what we think, what we feel, and what we see are true.

When we are in denial, we are living inside a self-made illusion that narrows our vision. Let me give you an example. Imagine being in a beautiful, lush forest, with hundreds of different kinds of plants, trees, and flowers, and discovering that inside these hundreds of acres of beautiful landscaping is a small patch of dead trees. Fascinated, you take out your camera, focus the lens on this small part of the forest, and snap a picture that contains only the dead trees. You develop the picture, and then you go around showing all your friends and family the picture of the dead trees. After a while you forget the lushness of the entire forest and begin to believe that your picture reflects the real condition of the forest.

Denial causes us to focus only on what we want to see in order to protect ourselves from the entire truth. We are taught to look the other way, to point our finger, and to blame others for our problems. But the problem with this method of self-protection is that it leaves us stuck in the delusion that we are the saint and our partner is the sinner, that we are the victim and our partner is the abuser. It leaves us angry, resentful, and powerless over the circumstances of our lives. It cuts us off from the lushness of the forest and leaves us in the presence of the dying trees.

In the midst of a turbulent divorce most of us are not looking through clear eyes. We are seeing the situation through a distorted reality. To regain the big picture we need to breathe deeply and take the time to separate the facts of our present situation from our fears about what might happen in the future. I saw this clearly when I met Mary. At forty-three years old, she had been separated from her husband, Kevin, for almost a year. In one of her first declarations Mary informed me that she was no longer angry with her husband. She then went on to explain that he was abusive toward their children and that she would have to fight for sole custody to protect them.

In fact, Mary constantly complained about Kevin, telling me how dangerous he was and maintaining that he should not be allowed to be with their children. I wanted to explore the abuse that Mary had experienced with Kevin, but every time I asked her about it she'd recount the same incident: Kevin had yanked her daughter Angela by the arm and made her cry. After weeks of listening to her talk about what a terrible father Kevin was, I asked Mary to list all the times he had abused their children. Mary's list was short. In fact, though she hesitated to admit it, she could remember only two incidents. One was the time he yanked Angela's arm and the other incident that was driving her to a custody battle was told to her by a friend. Her friend said she witnessed Kevin yelling at their son, Kyle, after a soccer game. Mary had created other incidents in her mind that led her to believe that Kevin was abusive. She had even convinced herself that Kevin was abusing the children by dropping them off at a before-school program. And, of course, on top of these beliefs were all kinds of imagined incidents that she feared would happen to her children in the future.

I wanted to make sure Mary was looking at the entire picture, so I asked her to list the good things that Kevin had to offer as a father. It took a few weeks, and she could add only one or two items a week, but after a couple of months she finally had a list of eight positive attributes of Kevin as a father. Her list looked like this:

1. Kevin wants to spend time with his children weekly.

2. He likes to help the children do their homework.

3. He likes going to soccer practice, and he even coaches the soccer team occasionally.

4. He encourages them in all their after-school activities.

5. He's interested in science and brings enthusiasm to a subject that both his children loathe.

6. He likes to videotape and catalog pictures of the kids at special events. (Mary herself never did this.)

7. He likes to ski and play tennis and brings his kids along with him so that he can teach them these sports.

8. He shows the children more discipline.

As long as Mary focused on Kevin's temper, she was unable to see the entire picture. Her lawyers had warned her that she didn't have enough evidence to pursue a full custody order, but she was so trapped in her story that she couldn't see the forest for the trees. All Mary was able to focus on were a couple of dead trees inside Kevin's forest.

I'm not suggesting that abuse is okay or that you don't have a right to protect your children, but I am suggesting that when you're going through a separation you cannot always see the entire picture. You tend to focus, whether you want to or not, on what doesn't work and what is unacceptable. It's a sure bet that at some point all your unexpressed emotions and withheld communications will come out in some form or another. You'll project all your anger, regret, or resentment onto the person you once loved more than anyone.

It's important to remember that denial is a form of self-protection. Otherwise known as "Don't Even Notice I Am Lying," denial is built into our psyche. It acts as a shield so that we can go on with our lives. It shows up as rationalization and justification, and in our minds it's always the truth. It's amazing how easy it is to focus on the small picture, all the while believing that we're seeing the whole truth. But to be happy instead of right we must open up to the possibility that things aren't always what they seem.

Someone once told me a story of two traveling angels who stop to spend the night at the home of a wealthy family. When they arrive and ask for lodging for the night, the family is rude and refuses to let the angels stay in one of the home's many guest rooms. Instead, the angels are given a small space in a cold basement. As the angels make their bed on the hard floor, the older angel sees a hole in the wall and repairs it. When the younger angel asks the older angel why he repaired the wall when their hosts have been so unkind, the older angel replies, "Things aren't always what they seem."

The next night, after a long day of travel, the angels come to rest at the house of a very poor but very hospitable farmer and his wife. After sharing what little food they have, the couple insists that the angels sleep in their bed, where they can have a good night's rest. When the sun comes up the next morning, the angels find the farmer and his wife in tears. Their only cow, whose milk has been their sole source of income, is lying dead in the field.

The younger angel is infuriated and asks the older angel: "How could you have let this happen? The first couple had everything but gave very little, yet you helped them. The second family had little but was willing to share everything, and you let their cow die." With love and compassion the older angel replies, "Things aren't always what they seem. When we stayed in the basement of the mansion, I noticed there was gold stored in that hole in the wall. Since the couple was so obsessed with greed and unwilling to share their good fortune, I sealed the wall so that they couldn't find it. Then last night, as we slept in the farmer's bed, the angel of death came for his wife. I asked for mercy and gave him the cow instead. Things aren't always what they seem."

When we remember that there is an order to the Universe and that things aren't always what they seem, then we can look beyond our own agenda or ego. In most instances, as soon as we separate from our partner, our battle armor goes up and denial sets in. Yet it's imperative, especially if we have children, to explore all realities. We must step out of the reality of our own small selves and into the fullness and enormity of the big picture. The big picture includes the possibility that our partners are in our lives to bring us light and healing, even if we can't see it. It's only when we step into the light of divine order that we can accept where we are today.

People and circumstances are the way they are for a reason, and even though we may not be able to see the gifts of someone's bad temper, cheapness, or neglect, it may be just what we need to gain access to our own unique gift. Kevin's temper may provide the impetus his child needs to become a defender of children's rights. Your wife's indifference may be exactly the motivation you need to become more available to your children or to a future spouse. At this point all you need to do is to be willing to see the entire forest rather than a small patch of dead trees. Shifting from a combative stance to a receptive one, you must step out of the shadow of your drama and into the light of the facts.

HEALING ACTION STEPS

1. Create a quiet environment free from distractions. Take out a pen and a pad of paper and begin writing your divorce story, complete with all the drama and emotion you feel about the events that transpired. Use language that expresses your deepest, darkest feelings. This is not a time to censor yourself, to be kind, or to take responsibility for your actions. Give yourself permission to bring forth whatever needs to be said concerning yourself, your partner, and your divorce.

2. Make a list of the facts about your divorce, without any story, drama, or judgment.

3. Go back and read your divorce story. As you revisit each detail, ask yourself, "Is this fact or fiction?"

Chapter Two

DIVINE ORDER

What the caterpillar calls the end of the world,
the Master calls the butterfly.

RICHARD BACH, *ILLUSIONS*

The Law of Acceptance awakens us to the profound awareness that we are always evolving, whether we are aware of it or not. Our lives are divinely designed for each one of us to get exactly what we need to support our own unique evolutionary process. Until we understand that everything in God's world is exactly as it should be, perfect without flaws, we spend our lives wishing that people, places, and things were different. We get caught up in our own internal struggles against what is, which only leads us to more pain and suffering. When we step into the Law of Acceptance, we begin to see that everything happening at this moment is exactly as it should be. We discover that nothing in the world occurs by accident and that there are no coincidences. When we deny the perfection of the moment and the perfection of the Universe, we are doomed to live a life filled with fear, pain, and hopelessness. Denying the reality of our circumstances is a fight we cannot win.

As a young adult, I suffered deeply from the divorce of my own parents. No matter how many therapists I saw or how much introspection I did, the tears and sadness over the loss of my family remained just under the surface of my consciousness for over ten years.

At the time I could see no rhyme or reason for having to go through so much pain and such deep loss, but looking back now, I can see that the divorce in my family and my own divorce were very necessary parts of my own spiritual journey. These two major events led me to discover the root of my pain and showed me that my thoughts, beliefs, and behaviors all stemmed from my unhealed emotional wounds.

The universal intelligence that resides within us is connected to all that is and all that will be and knows exactly what we need to embrace the enormity of ourselves. What each of us needs to evolve and grow to reach the magnificence of our own unique self is already encoded within us. Filled with vital information, this code is our guide to discovering our most extraordinary self. This universal intelligence guides us to attract the people who are perfectly suited to help us experience the exact incidents and feelings we need out if we are to awaken to the highest expression of ourselves.

I had to marry Dan. It was the Universe's way of supporting me in realizing my potential and becoming self-actualized. I had to marry someone who would unconsciously lead me back to my childhood wounds—who would know how to frustrate me and push every button I had. I had to marry someone who wouldn't give me what I believed I needed. Everything Dan said, everything he did or didn't do, provided the perfect skewers to puncture the defenses covering my deeply concealed wounds. My divorce and all the pain surrounding it forced me to question who I was and what I was doing here. Today I can see that hidden behind the veil of many traumatic events was the path leading me to fulfill my destiny. I learned that there are many realities—those that we see, those that others see, and, of course, those that none of us can see.

This truth is beautifully illustrated in an old Sufi story about a farmer and his son. One day when the farmer goes out to feed his animals, he finds his only horse lying on the ground, dead. Soon, the whole village has heard the news, and neighbors come by to say, "We've heard the awful news; it's terrible that you lost your only horse." The farmer turns to his friends and says, "Maybe."

The next day, while the farmer is working the land, his son runs to tell him that he just captured a herd of wild horses. Again the villagers hear the farmer's news and come by, saying, "You're so lucky that you have been blessed with this entire herd of horses." Again the farmer's only reply is, "Maybe." A few days later, while trying to tame one of the wild horses, the farmer's son is thrown to the ground and his leg is broken. A neighbor hears of this accident and comes by to say, "What poor luck you're having, I'm terribly sorry." The farmer's only reply, once again, is, "Maybe." Many weeks go by, and the son is still lame. The emperor sends out his messengers to round up all the able-bodied boys in the nearby villages to fight a local battle. When they arrive at the farmer's house, they see that his son is injured and pass him by. The neighbors, who have all lost their sons in the battle, again come to the farmer's house and say, "You're so lucky to have your son home with you." Again the farmer replies, "Maybe."

As you can see, you never know how life will turn out or why particular events occur. The Law of Acceptance teaches us that we are always evolving, whether we are aware of it or not. What might look like the worst event that has ever befallen you could be part of a brilliantly designed plan that will lead you to a place of fulfillment, peace, and contentment. Accepting your circumstances instantly relieves you of your internal struggle and frees you to start seeing new possibilities.

Acceptance also means trust. Trusting is a difficult task when we are in the grip of emotional pain. But we must understand that there is more going on than we know. There is an underlying web that surrounds each of us, even if we can't see it. Woven into this web are many different possibilities for our lives. As we travel down the road of life, we are continually given a choice of which path we are going to take. Every event that happens contains the seed of limitless possibilities for our future.

In each moment many different futures are available to you. All of them are trying to lead you back to your divine nature. Some paths are easier than others. If you always choose from your lower self—from the part that is fearful, addicted, and discontented—you will continue to encounter mountains of pain and years of suffering. If you choose from your higher self, you are still likely to encounter many bumps along the way, but by accepting that whatever is going on is exactly what should be going on, you can stand in strength, knowing that you are not alone but in a sacred partnership with the Divine.

It is entirely up to each one of us to choose when we are going to dance with the Universe. There's an old saying: "Life is a school to the wise man and an enemy to the fool." If we choose to be the wise man or woman, we learn from our mistakes and gain strength from our shortcomings. We take the time to study and contemplate the events that led up to our current situation, and we use our newfound understandings to heal the wounds of our past. Then we can reclaim a piece of the great wisdom of this world. That wisdom inspires us to explore our different options, knowing that there is a very specific reason that we are standing in this exact place at this moment and time.

Divine guidance speaks to us through synchronistic events. We often don't realize why we feel compelled to make certain decisions or why we are excited about something one day and turned off by it the next. We may not know why we've been fired from a job or left by a mate. Yet looking back, we can often see how each person and event conspired to bring us to who we are at this moment.

It is often impossible to see the entire mountain when you are climbing it. While you're struggling over each ledge, you're thinking, *This is crazy. Why am I here? Who got me into this mess? Why am I doing this?* But once you get to the top, you can look down and see how far you've come and how great your accomplishment is.

When we start to notice and acknowledge the pattern of events that have led us to this moment, we begin living a conscious life. This connectedness, invisible to us, is called synchronicity. It is the magical language of life. Synchronicity is our trail map, our guide to life's possibilities. In this conscious awareness we can see beyond circumstances and realize the inner connectedness of the people and events in our lives. When we reinterpret those events through the prism of synchronicity, we are able to see the divine order of our own unique path.

My life can be seen as a grand exercise in accepting that things are always as they are meant to be. On the surface the events that led me to the work I do now seemed random and scattered. But each event and each circumstance had a purpose; each gave me new insights and moved me to a new level of understanding. My job was to accept each setback or accomplishment as part of a greater plan for me.

Looking back at the events that led up to my divorce, I can now see that there was a divine design. It began to unfold when I was still living in Florida, single, and half-owner of a successful retail store. Struggling to find meaning for my life, I attended numerous workshops, leadership trainings, and communication courses. I tried many different forms of therapy, read countless books, and listened to hour after hour of self-help tapes, trying to find inner peace. For years I had felt less than satisfied with my life. During this time of self-discovery I realized that I had a deep desire to move to California. Even though I didn't understand why I yearned to leave the city where all of my family and friends lived, I was committed to exploring my inner urges.

One day, while attending a three-day human growth workshop, I heard about an organization called Prison Possibilities. Something about this charity sparked an interest in me. Again I chose to follow my inner urge to see where it would lead me. For years I had talked about volunteering my time to an organization, but I had never made the effort to actually get involved. I discovered that this organization was committed to bringing "The Forum," a personal growth seminar, into the country's prison system. I decided to volunteer to assist and attended a seminar at a prison in Colorado. I was terrified of the commitment it required, but at the same time I understood that if I followed the opportunities that were being presented to me, I would probably be led somewhere outside the small reality in which I had been living.

As life would have it, the morning before I was going to leave for Colorado a serious offer was made to buy my retail business. For nearly two years I had tried desperately to sell my retail store, without success. The prospect of finally selling it was both thrilling and terrifying because now, although I would be a free woman, I would also be unemployed. This thought literally made me weak at the knees. I was so overwhelmed with emotion that I postponed my trip. For days I struggled between holding on to the business that had brought me so much success and security and letting go of it to pursue my deeper dream. In the end I knew I needed to trust the Universe to be my guide and lead me to the next destination of my journey. With my decision to pursue my dreams, I boarded a plane to Denver, Colorado.

On the morning of the second day of the course, a very handsome man came and sat next to me on a bench in the back where all the Prison Possibilities assistants were seated. He introduced himself to me as Rich, the president of the organization. The moment our eyes met I knew that my life would never be the same. We fell in love sitting on that bench in a prison, and to make a very long story short, four months later I let go, sold my business, packed my belongings, and moved from Florida to San Francisco to live with Rich.

For months I was astonished at the perfection of the events that had led me to the prison program and to my meeting with Rich. Suddenly I understood that if I stepped out of my ego and trusted in the underlying intelligence that orchestrates the Universe, I would be led to the exact place, to meet the perfect person, to teach me the precise lessons that I needed to learn, to make me the person I always wanted to be.

While living in the Bay Area I attended JFK University and began studying Consciousness Studies and Transpersonal Psychology. At thirty-four, I was finally going to achieve my goal of completing college. It took a series of synchronistic events to get me to the precise place I was intended for.

While attending school, I also began leading transformational seminars for Landmark Education with the dream of one day leading "The Forum" in prisons. Even though I thrived as a seminar leader, whenever I spoke to anyone in the organization about the possibility of one day leading "The Forum" in the prison system, no one in charge seemed to share that same vision for me. For months I struggled with my options, unwilling to accept the fact that no one was supporting me in my dream. Then one day a girlfriend called and convinced me that I was barking up the wrong tree, that the likelihood that I would lead "The Forum" in the prison system was slim.

I was so resistant to hearing what she had to say. I had my heart set on saving America and transforming all the prisoners in our jails. But deep inside I sensed she was probably right. For days I mulled over her words and was reminded of something that Inayat Kahn, a Sufi wisdom teacher, said: "If it's not right for them, it's not right for you, and if it's not right for you, it's not right for them." In his low, gentle voice he explained how everything is in perfect harmony and that when the Universe and circumstances don't support us in getting what we think we want, it's only because there is something better in store for us, something that supports us in ways we can't see. He explained that if we can't see the perfection, it's only because we are living under a veil of illusion and being guided by an agenda of our own. He assured us that ultimately we would see that circumstances were guiding us to another path that would lead us to a higher reality.

Landmark Education's lack of encouragement ultimately led me to explore other career possibilities. It took me months to accept the fact that it was time for me to move on. But as soon as I did, as soon as I began to separate myself from the organization, I began to see that my life's work would take on a different tone.

At the same time my relationship with Rich was coming to an end. My heart was sad because I desperately wanted to be married and have a child. We had come to an impasse and decided to go our separate ways. So once again I packed my bags, took my dreams, and moved on. With my boxes only half unpacked, I attended a five-day conference in Santa Clara, where I met Dan. We were both committed to a life of transformation and service. We spent hours discussing all the ways in which we could each make the world a better place. When Dan and I decided to get married, my heart was filled with joy and excitement. Finally, I had met the man of my dreams.

I moved to San Diego to be with Dan. I became pregnant right away and immediately began creating a home for our family. The first couple of months of my pregnancy were extremely difficult. I suffered daily from morning sickness, my nausea brought out the worst in me, and everything and everyone bothered me. I was unhappy in the town where we lived and missed my friends and family. Never had I felt so alone. The stress of moving, leaving my job and school, and being pregnant and newly married was more than our relationship could handle. Painfully, before our son Beau was one year old, Dan and I decided to separate.

Right before Dan and I split up I became extremely concerned about how I was going to make it on my own. It didn't seem possible to take care of Beau and pursue a new career at the same time. Then one day I was offered an opportunity to work with Dr. Deepak Chopra and the Chopra Center for Well Being, which happened to be located about three miles from my home. Working with Dr. Chopra had been a dream of mine since I first heard him speak in San Francisco. I began working closely with Dr. David Simon, the medical director of the Chopra Center, and developed the Shadow Process, a three-day emotional release seminar that is the foundation of the work I do today.

Dr. Simon and Dr. Chopra embraced me as family and supported me in refining my gifts. Again I stood amazed at the perfection of the Universe. Here I was, facing one of the biggest disappointments I could ever imagine, and simultaneously I was offered a chance to fulfill one of my biggest dreams.

After my divorce, when I needed to figure out how I could support myself, my sister Arielle asked me what I could do to make a contribution to humanity and support myself at the same time. I closed my eyes, and the first thought that came to my mind was to write a book about the emotional release work I was doing in my seminars at the Chopra Center. To my relief and amazement, *The Dark Side of the Light Chasers* was released the same month my alimony was to end. This showed me once again that if I trusted the Universe and followed my heart, I would be provided for.

Are all these events just coincidences or the expression of the magic of the Universe? There were times along the way when I didn't like what I was seeing. Whenever the circumstances went in a different direction than I desired I would have to practice the Law of Acceptance. The easiest way I found was to express out loud the truth of my situation. When I wanted to lead "The Forum" in the prison and I saw that wasn't going to happen, I would repeat over and over to myself, *I am not going to lead "The Forum" in the prison. I am not going to lead "The Forum" in the prison.* When my business was sold and I knew I would have to live on a budget, I continually repeated, *I am going to live on a budget. I am going to live on a budget.* Stating my undesired reality over and over enabled me to move out of denial and into acceptance.

I can look at each move, each breakup, and each opportunity and see that there were always other choices I could have made. There were different cities to live in, numerous organizations to volunteer for, and a variety of different men to hang out with. At every turn there were different paths I could have chosen. Each person I've met, and every feeling I've felt, has in some way guided me to where I am today. Sitting here at my computer, I can honestly say that I wouldn't trade my life with anyone. So again I have the choice to either acknowledge the Universe for its magnificence or keep the blinders over my eyes and pretend that life just happens.

Once we look at the world through the eyes of acceptance, we can decide to open up to the perfection of our lives and begin to see why certain events are happening and why certain people have been brought into our world. Marcel Proust said, "The real voyage of discovery consists not in seeking new landscapes but in having new eyes." New eyes allow us to see all people and all events as our guides leading us to the exact right place we are supposed to be in in order to express our own personal and unique gift on this planet.

When we accept divine order, we begin to move more easily, to go with the flow of things, trusting that the river of life will take us where we need to go. We trust that although we can't see where we're going at this moment, we will arrive in a safe, more secure place than where we started. The alternative to accepting the divine order in our present circumstances is seeing our lives through the eyes of our ego.

When our life is being controlled by our ego, instead of floating with the natural flow of the river we get pulled by the guide of our lower self, and separateness becomes our map. This becomes a long, bumpy trip upstream when the river is flowing down.

When we are operating from the level of our ego, we live in fear, trying to protect ourselves from loss. We ask, *Why is this happening to me?* We think we are being mistreated and fear that someone is trying to take something away from us. In contrast to the viewpoint of our higher self, our ego does not have the big picture. Its function is to protect us as individuals, to look at all things from the perspective of "me." The ego says, "I'm not you. I'm different from you, and if I'm not careful you're going to hurt me." Our higher self says, "I am you. And if something is not working for you, it's not working for me." Even though you can't see the perfection of your life, you can trust the Law of Acceptance to remind you that you are right where you are meant to be. You can begin practicing trust by looking for clues that everything that is happening is serving a divine purpose. And that purpose is to awaken and guide you on your journey.

In the midst of our pain and confusion it is difficult to imagine where all this mess is leading us. Our lower self falls prey to our negative programming and limits what we can see. This was certainly true for Patrick and Jenny. One day Jenny came home from work nervous and upset and proceeded to tell her husband, Patrick, that she was dissatisfied with their marriage. With pain in her eyes, Jenny confessed to Patrick that her discontent had led her into a relationship with a man she had met at work. Patrick was both hurt and confused. The shocking news of his wife's betrayal left him frozen in fear, and for the first time in his life Patrick was emotionally devastated.

After many weeks and many tearful conversations, Jenny decided that she needed time to find herself and asked Patrick to move out of the house. When he declined, Jenny decided that she would move into an apartment, leaving Patrick in their house with their two children.

Patrick became deeply depressed. Initially it was difficult for him to stay focused at work and to take care of his children. But he worked hard to hold things together for the children, whom he now had in his custody for most of the time.

In the early years of his marriage Patrick was financially irresponsible and got the family into a lot of debt. Jenny was never able to resolve her anger and resentment toward Patrick. Caught up in the busyness of their lives, she had little time to deal with her emotions. Jenny never felt strong enough to face the problems that had plagued them for years, so she took on the role of micromanaging Patrick's behavior. Patrick took on a passive-victim role, just going along with whatever Jenny wanted. Not trusting Patrick's judgment, Jenny managed all of the finances and kept him on a tight budget. They became comfortable in their roles, and both of them succumbed to living a life of "quiet desperation."

While Patrick was suffering from the loss of his marriage, Jenny was off with her new love, exploring life as a single woman and feeling free for the first time in twenty years. Feeling powerless over Jenny's behavior, Patrick was now trying every way he knew to make himself stronger and to reach out for help. He began practicing acceptance, knowing that there was no other way out. Knowing there had to be a reason behind what was happening, he repeated this affirmation daily to give him the courage to move on: "God never gives me more than I can handle."

A few months later Patrick received a call at work from a woman who lived across the country. Amy couldn't remember where she had gotten Patrick's phone number, but she was interested in finding out more about some work he was doing in his job as a lobbyist for health care reform. Amy and Patrick quickly became phone friends. He felt close to her right away and looked forward to their daily phone conversations. Soon Patrick was confiding his personal problems to Amy.

This new friendship helped fill in part of the hole that he felt inside. He still suffered from a broken heart and was unable to reconcile his feelings toward Jenny. Every day he tried to convince himself that he was going to be all right and that he was strong enough to make it through the upheaval. But the pain was deep, and every time he thought of his wife being off with another man, he felt a knife stabbing away at his heart. Even with his immense love for his children, Patrick found it difficult to get out of bed and had little to look forward to in his daily life. The only light in his dark world became his daily phone conversations with Amy.

In a moment of excitement Amy and Patrick decided to meet near the city where she lived. When Patrick walked off the plane and saw Amy sitting there waiting for him, he knew his luck had changed. His heart opened, and for the first time in many months Patrick felt that he was going to be okay. Amy and Patrick spent a great weekend together, talking about their lives and noticing how much they had in common. Amy was a great cheerleader for Patrick, constantly affirming that he was going to be fine. She spent hours with him, listening to his pain and his fears. She began encouraging him to look beyond his current situation and supported him in remembering his dreams. For the first time in ten years Patrick was beginning to believe in himself again.

Meanwhile, Jenny had decided that she needed to move back into their house and that it would be best for Patrick to move into the apartment she had rented. Patrick agreed. Less than a year later Jenny and Patrick were officially divorced. Now Patrick was faced with the challenge of earning enough money to take care of himself and his child support responsibilities. Amy convinced Patrick that he could be a great success in business, and she made a commitment to stand by his side while he took the risk of leaving his job, in which he earned less than $40,000 a year, and starting his own company. With Amy's support, he knew he could do anything. Amy and Patrick decided to get married, and Amy moved her belongings into Patrick's apartment.

Looking back through the crisis, fear, hopelessness, and pain, Patrick will tell you how perfect each and every event was. Four years later Patrick's business has reached a level of success far beyond his projected goals. Instead of being continually reminded of his past failings, Patrick now enjoys a life based on the present and a future filled with extraordinary opportunities. At the age of forty-seven, he is finally fulfilling his childhood dream of being a success and earning more money than he ever imagined. He is grateful and feels in total alignment with his soul's purpose. Amy and Patrick now have a son of their own and are busy creating the life of their dreams. Jenny also remarried, and both families are thriving.

By stepping outside our personal expectations and judgments about how our lives should look, we gain access to the many possibilities that exist for us in the Universe. It's only when we get in our own way, when we are trying to decide all on our own what is right and what is wrong, that we stop the natural flow of our personal evolution.

There is a magnificent, unique design for each of our lives hidden behind the veil of our sometimes turbulent experiences. The Universe provides us with many opportunities to unfold our personal roadmap to happiness. All we have to do is let go and let God.

HEALING ACTION STEPS

1. Make a list of five difficult experiences you have had. Next to each one, write one lesson that you learned as a result of it. How has that lesson helped you in your life?

2. List twenty favorable things that have come out of your separation from your partner. As the following list suggests, the benefits of your breakup may be significant or quite superficial. It may be helpful to look to your grievances for inspiration. If you are unable to find any, ask friends and family to help you. Your list might look something like this:

- I don't have to share the bathroom.
- I have more time for reading and self-reflection.
- I can be myself without having to please someone else.
- I don't have to make dinner anymore.

- I don't have to answer to anybody regarding my comings and goings.

- I feel free to go back to school.

- I can invite friends and family over any time of the day or night.

THE LAW OF
SURRENDER

Chapter Three

THE PATH OF LEAST RESISTANCE

We turn to God for help when our foundations are shaking,
only to learn that it is God who is shaking them.

CHARLES C. WEST

The Law of Surrender tells us that when we stop resisting and surrender to our situation exactly as it is, things begin to change. We resist out of the fear that if we let go, we will be faced with circumstances we can't handle. Our resistance is a natural protective mechanism, a shield that we unconsciously put up to guard ourselves against pain. We live in the illusion that this shield will somehow protect us from feeling the loss, guilt, distress, and anguish of our current situation. But in the end resistance doesn't protect us as much as it robs us of our right to heal. Our resistance prevents us from seeing what's so, what's true, and what's possible for our lives. When we surrender, we let go of our pictures of how life should be and allow ourselves to be in the presence of our life exactly as it is, without any interpretation or illusion.

A year after my divorce I experienced firsthand the grip of resistance. One day, during a phone conversation with Dan, he began questioning my financial situation. He asked me about the projects I was working on and how much money I was making from each of them. By the time I got off the phone my hands were sweating and I could feel the pressure in my chest and the tightness in my body. I had just bought a house that I could barely afford, and I feared that Dan wanted to decrease his child support payments. Looking back, I could see that when I spoke to Dan about money, I was covering up how much I was making. I minimized my success and overdramatized my financial condition, as if I were putting on battle armor in preparation for the fight.

Then one night soon thereafter I woke up in the middle of this paranoid state and asked myself, *What is going on?* For weeks I had been living in fear, and I knew that I needed to surrender to my resistance. I knew that, to get rid of my anxiety, I had to get to the bottom of my fear and deal with the pain that surrounded my money issues. So I took out my journal and wrote, "If Dan lowered my child support, what would happen?"

1. I'd have less monthly income.

2. I wouldn't be able to afford my house.

3. I'd have to sell the house I just bought.

4. I'd have to rent instead of own.

5. I'd have to use the only money I have for my day-to-day living expenses.

6. I'd have to find another way to support myself.

At first I was horrified. I wanted desperately to be able to afford the house I had just bought. Tears came to my eyes, and I knew there must be a deeper issue. I looked beneath my initial response and saw that I just wanted to feel safe and to have a beautiful home for Beau and me to live in. I felt that at least I deserved that. I left my journal and went back to sleep.

When I woke up, I decided I had to handle the problem no matter what, so I looked over my list again. This time I realized that, if this was the worst of it, I could survive. I'd have less money, I'd be living in a rented apartment, and I'd be living off of my savings; the question that I would now need to answer would be: *In this new situation, how can I be happy and have a great life?*

Assuming the worst-case scenario and making my list enabled me to see that I could live with the worst outcome. I was then prepared to face what I perceived as Dan's attack. In the midst of this process I had a moment of clarity: I realized that if Dan didn't want to give me the amount of child support he was giving me—if I was going to have to fight, beg, or live in a hostile environment—then I didn't want it. I had to ask myself, *Do I want to live every day taking something from someone who is resenting me?* The answer for me was clearly no. I knew that not everyone was lucky enough to have this choice, but thankfully, I was. I decided that almost anything would be better than remaining dependent on someone who didn't want to support me.

When morning came, I nervously picked up the phone and called Dan. I told him I had the feeling he was questioning me about money because he was planning to lower his monthly child support payments. I told him of my discomfort since our last conversation, and then I said the words I never thought would come out of my mouth: "I appreciate receiving child support, but if it doesn't work for you to give me the amount you're giving me, I don't want to take it." I did tell him I'd probably have to sell my home, but it wasn't his problem; I would figure it out.

I stepped into my fear, I surrendered my resistance, and to my great surprise, Dan said, "I wasn't asking those questions for that reason. I was just wondering how you were paying your bills." He then expressed his desire to contribute financially to our support and said it was important to him for Beau to have a nice home. When I had imagined Dan withholding child support, I feared that I would never be able to make it on my own. Only by being willing to embrace my deepest fears did I discover that the worst outcome wouldn't ruin my life.

THE PAIN OF RESISTANCE

Resistance locks us inside of the emotional pain of a situation. It traps us in the reality that we most want to change. Resistance comes from wishing or wanting our present reality to be different. Resistance causes stress. Imagine that I'm going to hit you and allow yourself to tense up in anticipation. Now feel the tightness within your body. This response is exactly what occurs within our bodies when we resist any person or situation.

Resistance locks us into our own will by denying other realities. Living in the confines of our personal will, we feel separate and alone. When we are locked into our personal will, we are living in an internal conversation that revolves around the thought, *It shouldn't be like this.* We then spend all our energy trying to change the outer reality of our circumstances. Internally conflicted, we struggle to make sense of our situation and fight to control our partner's behavior.

Surrendering goes against our natural reaction to fight for our rights and hold on to what we believe is ours. But until we surrender, we are glued to the pain of our breakup. Surrendering is especially difficult if we've been betrayed, abandoned, or deceived. But if we accept that everything is happening exactly as it should, we can begin to surrender and trust in the natural flow of the Universe. To transcend our suffering we must go against our instinct to hold on and instead surrender to the path of letting go.

In my studies of Tang Soo Do, a form of Korean karate, my teacher, Master John Gehosky, has taught me that sometimes the best way out of a compromising position is to let go. For example, if an attacker grabs my arm, instead of tightening up and pulling away, I need to step toward my opponent and relax my arm completely. Pulling away from my attacker triggers a natural response in him to hold on tighter. To get away from my attacker, I must first surrender to his grip. When I let go and relax, my opponent's grip naturally loosens, giving me the opportunity to break free from his hold. My initial response is always to resist any perceived threat. Yet it's only when I breathe deeply, relax, and lean into the experience that I stand strong and gain access to all my power and strength.

Anything you want to change, anything you're afraid of, anything you refuse to accept causes internal resistance. If you resist your husband's upsetting communications, then he will keep trying to communicate the same thing over and over again until he is heard. If he senses that you will never receive his communications, he may choose to shut down and to communicate his upset covertly, in a passive-aggressive way. But if you loosen the grip of your expectations, breathe deeply, and open yourself to what he is going to say, you can listen from a place of surrender. Listening from a place of surrender requires that you soften your heart, let go of your expectations, and listen with innocent ears. You then grant him the right to his opinions and feelings. Then you're able to receive his communication without defense, without resistance. You are allowing him to be heard, and being heard is often all that an individual needs in order to let go of an upset. Then you can both put away your armor and let go of your defensive stance.

To listen from a place of surrender is to relinquish all your judgments for the moment. You give up the notion that you are right and the belief that you know what he's going to say. Then you step into a quiet place, into a bigger view of the Universe, recognizing that what's going on with your partner may not be personal. This offers him the freedom to communicate freely. But when you resist hearing his truth, you remain stuck, glued to the very thing you want to get away from.

THE POWER OF SURRENDER

When we surrender, we say, "This is what life is dealing me right now, and even though I'd like it to be different, I will allow it to be as it is." We give up our attachment to how we want our lives to be and how we want our partner to be. When we're attached to something, we resist any outcome different from the one we want, as well as any behaviors or feelings that don't fit into our perceived pictures. Any time something other than our desired result shows up, resistance comes right along with it. Then we immediately seek to change the circumstances to fit into our desired reality, and when we can't do that, we become angry, resentful, frustrated, or sad.

In the sacred state of surrender we are able to detach from the outcome. To enter into this sacred state we must keep affirming in every moment the perfection of the Universe. We must remind ourselves that there is a divine order and that everything is exactly as it is meant to be. When we find ourselves resisting, controlling, or holding on, we must breathe deeply and with each exhalation affirm that it is safe to let go of our limited perspective. It is safe to let go of our marriages.

The payoffs we receive from surrendering are extraordinary. When we surrender our will, we gain the freedom to be in the present moment, and only when we are living in the present moment are we able to see all of our choices—even the ones that may have previously been hidden from us. Surrender gives us the gift of peace of mind and trust in the benevolence of the Universe.

Surrender is an act of courage. It is a divine path that gives us access to realities beyond what we already know. To surrender is to acknowledge the divine nature of the Universe and affirm that the Universe has our happiness in its heart. Surrender encourages us to step out of the personal realm—the part of us that feels separate and alone—and step into the universal realm where we are all interconnected.

Even though we are all uniquely different in our outer expression, we are very much the same in our inner world. Though it appears that we stand alone, there is another reality in which we are all part of a greater whole. Our perceived separateness is an illusion. It's a cosmic joke that tricks us into believing that you and I are independent of each other, that my actions are mine and yours are yours.

Take a moment and consider the possibility that our separateness is just an illusion. What if we are truly interconnected? Would you still try to make things turn out your way at the expense of others? Would you take everything that is said and unsaid so personally? Would your self-determination be your guide to peace and contentment?

AN EXPANDED PERSPECTIVE

The Yoga Vasistha, an ancient Hindu text, describes us as being very much like the ocean. When we gaze out at the ocean, we see countless waves—each one a different expression within a huge body of water.

Imagine each ripple, each wave, thinking that it is separate from the rest. A big wave may fear that it's too big, while a small wave suffers in the belief that it's too small. One wave presumes it's too warm, while another thinks it's too cold. Because they believe themselves to be separate from the ocean and from each other, each wave, ripple, and riptide fears the end of its existence when it crashes against the shore.

Now take a moment and picture each wave trying desperately to take the ocean in its own direction. Imagine that every time a wave happens to overlap another wave, or causes it to crash upon the shore, the wave that got hit files a lawsuit or pouts, refusing to return to the ocean. Imagine two beautiful waves joining together and giving birth to three little waves. In time, as the tides shift and the two waves begin to move in opposite directions, what if instead of supporting the little waves in becoming stronger, bigger, and more independent, the larger waves splash and crash into each other? Imagine that each one is concerned only with pulling the little ones along with it. Think about what ocean life would be like if each wave thought of itself as separate from the rest and used its will for its own personal benefit. How would it be if each wave took itself seriously, or took the other waves' actions personally? What would it be like if every wave stopped going with the natural flow of the tides? What would happen if every time the winds shifted and began moving the water in a different direction, all the waves started putting up a fuss?

When you look out at the ocean, it's almost impossible to see each wave as a separate entity; we naturally see everything contained within this body of water because we are taught to view it this way. To heal we must each realize that we are like the waves in the ocean. It may appear that we are separate, because that's what most of us have been told, but like each wave that crashes against the shore, we will all ultimately dissolve back into the universal mind, reuniting with the collective energy of the Universe.

Seeing how you're part of a bigger picture allows you to experience yourself beyond your ego, beyond your personal agenda, beyond your limited views of your life and of the world. Holding a larger perspective allows you to see the enormity of your true nature and propels you into the universal realm. When you realize the vastness of who you are—the entire ocean rather than a separate wave—you begin to trust in the magnificence of the Universe again. Trust is the key that enables you to surrender your will to this truth.

TRANSCENDING THE EGO

In order to trust again, we have to look at the natural order of life. This is the only way we can transcend our ego. Our ego is an important aspect of ourselves, but we must remember that its job is to make us uniquely ourselves, to mark us as separate individuals. The definition of the ego is "self" distinguished from "other." *I*, *me,* and *my* all constitute the self. Our egos fight fiercely to maintain control, always taking things personally, always trying to re-create some ideal or image from the past. It's the ego that continually reminds us of all the ways our partner hurt or misled us. And our ego is quick to expose our partner's deceit and indiscretions. While caught in the trap of our ego, we are doomed to replay our mistakes and personal shortcomings over and over again. Anyone whose mind is filled with the self-righteous negative chatter of his or her ego can attest that it feels like an involuntary form of self-torture.

Surrendering is a difficult task for the ego. To our fear-based ego surrender feels wrong. In a society where everyone is desperately fighting to be different, independent, and strong, surrender is often viewed as a sign of weakness or stupidity. We're taught to stand up and fight, to be right at all costs. We're told that leaders are strong and followers are weak. We're taught to be leery of the other guy, and we come to believe that if we don't fight, we may not have enough love, money, or time with our children.

The fight-or-flight reaction is the initial response of the ego: "I will get back at you, or I will withdraw from you." Both are protection mechanisms designed to shield us from going deeper inside to the core of the problem, to the core of our pain. Left unhealed, anger, hurt, betrayal, fear, paranoia, loss, and frustration become the negative chatter that continually tells you that you're right and everyone else is wrong. You may be hearing, *This can't be, This isn't fair,* or, *This is not what is supposed to happen,* so you struggle desperately to reconcile the situation within yourself. Or, if you initiated the separation, you may be feeling guilty about what you have done. You may be hearing, *I shouldn't have done this, Look at all the people I hurt,* or, *I've ruined everything.*

Inside your mind you continually bump up against a wall of unfulfilled expectations, disappointments, and old upsets that tell you, *This is not how I planned my life, It's not supposed to look this way,* and, *It's certainly not supposed to feel this way.* All the pictures from our past of how we wanted our lives or our partners to be make it difficult for us to surrender. In an attempt to protect ourselves from pain, we often avoid the entire truth about ourselves. This leads us right into the depths of suffering. Dr. Spencer Johnson, author of *The Precious Present,* said: "Suffering is simply the difference between what is and what I want it to be."

EMBRACING THE UNKNOWN

In Deepak Chopra's best-selling book *The Seven Spiritual Laws of Success,* he writes:

> *In detachment lies the wisdom of uncertainty . . . in the wisdom of uncertainty lies the freedom from our past, from the known, which is the prison of past conditioning. And in our willingness to step into the unknown, the field of all possibilities, we surrender ourselves to the creative mind that orchestrates the dance of the universe.*

Fear of the unknown, fear of doing without, and fear of the future prevent us from detaching. We may believe that if we hold on tighter to our money, our children, our resentments, or our opinions, we'll be able to control our world. In times of trauma it's a natural response to be afraid and hold on, thinking that's the only way we can sway the outcome in the direction we most desire. But fear—and all control issues are fear-based—is a sure recipe for pain and suffering.

Once we're willing to detach from our circumstances, we begin to experience the feeling of freedom again. The constant drain of having to have things turn out "our way" stops. The huge weight we carry on our shoulders melts away, and we begin to experience the power of our authentic nature. When we stop trying to move the ocean in our direction, we experience life with the ease of a surfer riding a wave.

Detachment doesn't mean giving up your intention to have things be different. It means relinquishing the results to the Divine, to the Universe, to a Power greater than yourself, so that this Power can orchestrate the unfolding of a plan that holds everyone's highest good. Detachment means living in the moment and being okay with the uncertainty of the future.

When I met Natalie, she had just finished her master's degree and was working to build a private practice as a psychotherapist. Natalie struggled with the issue of never being able to meet her financial goals. One day during one of our talks Natalie informed me that her ex-husband, Matthew, from whom she had been divorced for over eleven years, was still paying her bills. This seemed odd to me: Natalie had no children and had been married for only a few years. I sensed that Natalie was embarrassed by this disclosure, so I asked her how she felt about taking money from Matthew. She admitted that she didn't like it, but she was caught in a difficult situation and was convinced that there was no way she could pay her bills without Matthew's support.

For the next couple of months Natalie and I worked together to explore her fears around money and her crippling belief that she couldn't make it without a man. When we finally got to the core of the issue, Natalie realized that she had no faith and no trust. She believed that if she didn't squeeze money out of Matthew, she would end up homeless on the street. Natalie knew that her financial needs were draining her ex-husband, but she also knew that he was such a nice guy he would never deny her money. Knowingly taking advantage of Matthew only added to her feelings of low self-worth. Natalie's lack of trust and her unwillingness to surrender chained her to the very thing that stood in the way of her happiness.

Then one day Natalie decided that she didn't want to hold on any longer. She wanted to get on with her life and make room for a new partner to show up. Natalie told me, "I want God to be my partner instead of a man." Natalie knew she had to break out of the cocoon of her ex-husband if she was ever going to overcome her fear that she couldn't survive on her own. With great apprehension, she set a date a couple of months later, picked up the phone, and informed Matthew that on July 1 he would no longer have to send her money.

Sweating and shaking, Natalie acknowledged her quantum leap, her first step in reclaiming her power. When July 1 came, she never even noticed that the check had not arrived. She had been so busy marketing herself to other therapists, building her clientele, and practicing her new habit of letting go that she forgot about her need for help. In the next year Natalie went from making $26,000 to over $80,000 in her private practice. She went from running small races to fulfilling her dream of running the Boston Marathon. Natalie excelled in her work and gained the freedom she longed for in every area of her life. Finally she was a free woman trusting in the divinity of the Universe.

Letting go and detaching propelled Natalie into her own power. In a letter she wrote, "Once I let go and detached from my childhood beliefs, I found my power. Now I know God." Surrendering allowed Natalie to trust in the natural flow of the Universe and to reclaim her authentic power, which opened up a whole new world of possibilities.

TRUSTING THE PROCESS

Divorce is a process of letting go. For some people it happens in the first year; for others it takes longer. The Universe is there guiding us, and if we allow it, we will be taken care of. If we veer away from this truth, we will always live in fear, holding on to whatever we think will bring us security.

My friend Gerhard compares the process of divorce to his sailing adventures. One day he set off to sail from the land he knew to a small, distant island. For a few hours, whenever he looked back, he was able to see the land he had left behind. But the further he sailed, the smaller his homeland became, until it finally faded into the distant ocean. Now he could no longer see the place he had left behind, and the island he was traveling to was still out of sight. Feeling lost, he looked into the water for direction. He had been taught that instead of looking for the faraway place, you must look into the water. When you look into the water, you know the boat is moving and you're making your way.

When you are too focused on the outcome, you may panic and miss the fact that you are making progress step by step. When you have drifted from the safety of your past and your future is not yet on the horizon, you can experience deep loneliness and feel lost, floating in a sea of turbulent feelings. Likewise, when you detach from the outer world, you let go of your self-determination and your will. Detachment is a state of effortless flow. It's a place where uncertainty and the unknown share a graceful dance. It's a place where we can find peace in the perfectly imperfect.

We know from all the great sages that we're a perfectly designed species and our birthright is to experience peace and contentment. The outer world is our chalkboard, our playground, and if we don't like the way it looks or feels we can go back to the drawing board and begin again. All outer possessions are temporary, whether it's the love of our partner, our home, our status in society, or our career. As long as we're attached, we are slaves, nothing but prisoners of our desires and hostages to what we've deemed important. We are handcuffed to everything we're attached to, dragging our desires and dislikes with us wherever we go.

It's not until we can let go and detach from the outcome that we align with the highest good of our souls. Then, when the tides shift, moving us in an unfamiliar direction, we remain strong and safe, grounded in the knowledge that no matter how turbulent the wave, we can flow back into the warmth and comfort of the ocean. It's then that we discover the peace and contentment that reside deep at the core of our being. We enjoy the safety of knowing that everything we need to fulfill ourselves is right here within us. Having faith and trust that we are part of this bigger whole allows us to surrender. Our trust in the Universe is a floor of stability beneath our feet. It leaves us bathed in the wisdom that our lives are unfolding as they should be and that the Universe has a plan for each one of us. When we surrender, we let go of our resistance to what is happening in our lives. Surrender is the ultimate sign of strength and the foundation for a spiritual life.

Surrendering affirms that we are no longer willing to live in pain. It expresses a deep desire to transcend our struggles and transform our negative emotions. It commands a life beyond our egos, beyond that part of ourselves that is continually reminding us that we are separate, different, and alone. Surrendering allows us to return to our true nature and move effortlessly through the cosmic dance called life. It's a powerful statement that proclaims the perfect order of the Universe.

When you surrender your will, you are saying: "Even though things are not exactly how I'd like them to be, I will face my reality. I will look it directly in the eye and allow it to be here." Surrender and serenity are synonymous; you can't experience one without the other. So if it's serenity you're searching for, it's close by. All you have to do is resign as General Manager of the Universe. Choose to trust that there is a greater plan for you and that if you surrender, it will be unfolded in time.

Surrender is a gift that you can give yourself. It's an act of faith. It's saying that even though I can't see where this river is flowing, I trust it will take me in the right direction.

HEALING ACTION STEPS

It's important that you bring your full attention to these exercises. All the answers you need are inside of you; you only have to become quiet enough to hear them. Leave yourself plenty of time and completely surrender to the process. You may want to light some candles, put on some soft music, and create a nurturing atmosphere. Have your journal and a pen nearby.

1. When you are ready, close your eyes and take five slow, deep breaths. Use your breath to relax your body and quiet your mind. Now, with your eyes closed, ask yourself the following questions. Write the answers down in your journal.

- What am I resisting in my life?

- What am I afraid of?

- What will happen if I surrender to the situation?

- What am I getting out of holding on to the resistance?

- Who is getting hurt?

- What obstacles need to be removed before I can surrender?

2. The purpose of this exercise is to identify your fears, imagine the worst possible outcome, and discover what you could do to turn the situation around so that it empowers you. Prepare yourself by setting aside approximately half an hour of quiet, uninterrupted time. Have your journal and a pen nearby. Light a candle and say a prayer asking for the courage to face your worst fears. Now take three slow, deep, centering breaths, inhaling through your nose and exhaling through your mouth. When you are calm and relaxed, ask yourself these questions, choosing one situation at a time.

- What is my worst fear about what is happening in my life right now?

- With this fear, what is the worst possible outcome that could happen?

3. Make a list of your worst fears without editing them. Looking at the worst possible outcome, imagine that what you've feared has come true. Now ask yourself these questions:

- Now that this has happened, what do I need to do to be happy?
- What steps do I need to take?
- Who do I need to contact?
- Where do I need to go?
- What do I need to change?

When we can be at peace with the worst possible outcome, we are free.

4. Make a list of all the things you dislike about the separation process.

5. Write a new version of your divorce story in which you exaggerate the facts and your feelings, making them fifty times worse.

THE LAW OF

DIVINE
GUIDANCE

Chapter Four

YOU ARE NOT ALONE

You can't see the angel, you can't see the air.
You can't see my love for you, but it is everywhere.

ANONYMOUS

The Law of Divine Guidance shows you that God will do for you what you cannot do for yourself. Once you surrender your small ego to the larger plan of divine guidance, the defenses you have used to protect yourself from your ex-spouse will no longer be necessary. When we finally surrender our picture of how things should be, we make ourselves available for a new reality to emerge. Standing in the presence of divine guidance, we become humble; our pride is replaced by openness and a willingness to learn. This humility is the doorway through which the Divine can walk into our lives. Without humility, we believe that we can do it ourselves. Without humility, our false sense of pride, or ego, prohibits us from seeing the entire situation with clear eyes. Our egos remain in charge until we step outside our righteous belief that we are independent and separate beings. As long as this myth is intact, we keep the door closed to our higher wisdom.

Though it may not seem like it, divorce is an opportunity to rest in and count on our Divine Creator. Meditation and prayer quiet our minds, soothe our emotions, and support us in returning to the hope and excitement we had as children. Negative emotions come to remind us that we've slipped out of this place of innocence and into a cloud of fear. Our fears are made up of our anger, pain, worries, resentment, and emotional distress, while our faith is made up of hope, possibility, trust, and an inner belief in the benevolence of the Universe. Fear and faith cannot coexist. Fear shuts us down, while faith opens us up.

When we have faith, we know that even though we may not see light or good at this moment, it will come. Faith lets us know that there is something outside of ourselves that will guide and support us. Faith opens the door to new understandings and new views and gives us access to the wisdom of the ages.

In the middle of my separation from Dan, my sister Arielle came over to see how I was doing. I was in the midst of one of my emotional outbursts—feeling lost, lonely, and terrified that I couldn't make it on my own. Arielle asked me to sit down and close my eyes. She then asked, "What are you afraid of?" I repeated this question over and over again in my mind. Before long I was overcome with the feeling that I was completely alone and that there was nobody to help me. In that moment I felt all the other times in my life when I had been left alone and in pain. It felt like a knife was jabbing into an open wound on my chest. I could barely breathe. My sadness was so deep that it blinded me to any other realities. My biggest fear had surfaced. I believed that I would be stuck forever in the empty, painful feelings of my loneliness.

Arielle held me close as I cried, allowing my sadness to express itself. She then told me that fear is nothing more than forgetting that everything is all right. She reminded me that even in this moment of despair, a Divine Presence was here with us. If I wanted help, all I needed to do was close my eyes and ask. For a few minutes we sat side by side and prayed that I would find my faith again—that I would experience a shift in consciousness so big that I would know that I've never been alone and that I will never be alone again. All I needed to do, moment by moment, was remember that this Presence is with me.

Instantly I knew that despite outer appearances I never had to walk alone.

Our separation from our mate exposes the emptiness within us. Most of us thought that marriage would make us whole. And now, in the breakdown of our union, we are left feeling incomplete, lost, alone, flawed, and confused. We believe that our tears of sadness, walls of resignation, and cries of pain are caused by the collapse of our marriage, but there is more going on than we know. Much of our pain stems from our disconnection not just from our mate but from our Divine Mother, our Creator.

Sarah had been dependent on her husband for her emotional and spiritual well-being for many years. When I met her, she had been separated for twelve months from the man she had deemed to be the love of her life. There were many days when Sarah was consumed by her loneliness. Feeling broken and alone, she would sink into bouts of depression that often lasted for weeks.

Her hopelessness caused Sarah to reach out for help, to go back to church, and to spend hours reading self-help books. On a conscious level she knew that there was a power somewhere that could help her, because she had experienced a few days and hours of feeling hopeful and safe during this dark time. But Sarah could not seem to hold on to the good feelings. She kept getting caught in her negative self-chatter, which repeatedly told her that it was her fault her marriage had ended and that if she had paid more attention to her husband and done the things he asked, she would still have the one thing in the world that she loved. Her negative self-talk shut her off from the greater power that could help her. Though she had moments of clarity, she inevitably fell back into the trap of her disconnected, discontented ego.

When I asked Sarah what had inspired her feeling of hope and peace, she realized that the feeling arose when something or someone reminded her that she was trying to do it all alone—that she was trying to sail the ship in the direction she desired but had left the crew on the shore instead of taking the support she needed with her. Sarah needed only gentle reminders to remember that she wasn't in charge of navigating the ship and she didn't have to sail it all alone. If she wanted the full team of support available to her, all she needed to do was to fill her mind with prayer and she would be lifted from the pain of depression into the light of hope.

Divorce pushes us back into the small, broken shell of our ego, but to have a complete and total healing we must find our way back into the arms of the Divine. To experience our divinity on the deepest level we must stop listening to the noisy internal chatter that occupies our minds. Rama Berch, director of the Master Yoga Academy, once told me, "I don't allow my mind to think a thought without my permission." We must remember that this internal negative chatter is not us, and that we are the only ones who have the power to decide to stop listening to it.

When we recognize that we are trapped in the little voice of our ego, we can stop for a moment, close our eyes, take a few slow, very deep breaths, and shift our thoughts to a higher plane of consciousness. We must shine the light of our higher self on the negative chatter of our lower self by saying out loud, "I will no longer spend my time and energy listening to doubt, fear, and self-condemnation." We must affirm that this chatter does not reflect the part of us that is connected to God or a higher power but rather is the voice of the part of us that is separate, alone, and wounded. Once we understand that we don't have to listen to our doubts and fears, we can open ourselves up to receiving the Law of Divine Guidance, which affirms that God will do for us what we cannot do for ourselves, and that our egos will remain in charge until we step outside our righteous belief that we are independent and separate beings.

When we remember that we are not alone, we can begin to trust that if we let go of our partner, there will be something bigger there for us to rest upon. Even if you have been the major contributor to the breakdown of your marriage, you still deserve to heal and reconnect with your higher power. Many of us are taught that if we're good people God will take care of us and if we're bad he won't. This is a lie.

God is always there waiting for you to surrender your will and your separateness so he can walk with you instead of behind you.

GETTING TO KNOW GOD

The God I speak of is not an all-powerful presence that lives outside of us, but rather a universal force that lives in the core of our being, connecting us to all that is and all that will be. It's an all-encompassing energy that is both powerful and wise, a force that is often referred to as spirit, love, universal consciousness, divine order, or nature. It is known by many names, and there are many paths that can lead you to the God presence within. To begin, all you need is an honest desire to know God and an openness to have this force guide you to right action.

In his book *The Power of Constructive Thinking*, Emmett Fox teaches us that God is our own knowledge of the truth and that knowledge of the truth is in itself the Presence of God. But it's not intellectual knowledge that he speaks of—it's the actual experience of God. Not a knowing of our heads but an experience of our hearts. Our intellectual knowledge of God often prevents us from having the experience of God, because knowing in our minds actually limits the possibility of something greater.

At this stage, when we are recovering from the pain of separation, it is not surprising that we want to rely only on what we can see. We rely on our minds because our hearts have been so hurt. But intellectual knowing can shut the door to other possibilities and lock us into a set reality, preventing anything new from showing up. To grow past the hurt we need to experience the Divine beyond our intellects. We must trust that we are more than our doubt, fears, and negative thoughts. We are more than the mess of feelings we may be experiencing in this moment.

When we are willing to journey beyond what we are certain we know, we surrender to what the Buddhists call "beginner's mind."

Beginner's mind refers to the state of the innocent child, the state of wonder in which we lived before we developed set beliefs about the world. To return to this place of innocence we must relinquish what we know and let go of our judgments and beliefs. We must be willing to live in the uncertainty, in the unknowing of who we are and who God is. It is then that we become open and are able to move out of our heads and into our hearts.

In the beginning of my divorce I was sure that Dan would want to take my son away from me. Even though I had no evidence of any kind to support this thought, whenever I felt scared and alone, I would obsess over the possibility of a custody battle. After a couple of discussions with my friend Rachel, I realized that my fear of losing Beau, the only person I loved and could hold on to at that time, was being expressed through my obsession. Every time I thought about Dan taking Beau away from me, my heart raced and I was besieged with sadness. No matter what anyone said to me, I suffered alone at night with my negative thoughts.

After weeks of sinking deeper and deeper into my sadness, I remembered to ask for guidance. Even though I knew and believed I could be helped by my higher power, in the throes of my fears I always seemed to forget. So I took out a pad of little yellow stickies and started writing "God loves and protects me" on one after another. When I had gathered enough for every room in my house, I put them up everywhere so that I wouldn't forget. I put them in my purse and in my car, and every time the thought came into my mind that Dan would take Beau from me, I would breathe deeply and get myself back into a state of beginner's mind. I would remember that I didn't know how life would turn out and that I could control no one's behavior but my own. Then I would affirm out loud that God loves and protects me. I would repeat these words over and over again until I began to feel some relief.

After weeks of cultivating an attitude of not knowing and being open to receiving divine love and protection, I felt my fear drop away. Looking back now, I can see that there was no reality to my fears about Dan taking Beau. It was only my mind playing games with me. It had been my choice all along either to play in the game or to step outside of my mind to live in a reality of peace and security.

INVITING HELP IN

Healing comes when you have the courage and the humility to ask for help—this is an act of faith. Having faith is probably one of the most difficult states to achieve when you're filled with disappointment, sadness, anger, or regret. During these times we need faith that we'll find faith again. We need to remember times in our lives when we had faith, and when faith saw us through.

Faith is a state of complete trust. It affords us the knowledge that we are all connected and guided by a supreme intelligence that ultimately has our best interests in mind. Faith allows us to return to an authentic place of power where we trust that our lives will turn out in a positive way. Faith lives right behind the wall of fear that prevents us from living with an open heart. Faith is believing without a shadow of a doubt that the universe is good. It is faith that paves the way for angels and miracles to show up in our lives.

I once heard a story about a single mother named Julie with four young children. Her husband had just vanished from their lives, leaving her without any money. Julie knew that she had to find a job, so one cold, windy morning she put on her best dress and loaded her family into her truck. The five of them went to every factory, store, and restaurant in their small town. No luck. The kids stayed crammed into the truck, doing their best to be quiet, while Julie tried desperately to convince one employer after another that she was willing to learn or to do anything to have a job. Days passed, and still nothing turned up. The last place Julie tried was a truck stop a few miles out of town. The owner, an old lady named Granny, hired Julie to work the graveyard shift as a waitress. Julie would work from eleven at night until seven in the morning, for $4.65 an hour plus tips. Granny told her she could start that night.

Julie raced home and called the neighborhood teenager who baby-sat for her. She promised the girl that her children would already be asleep and that she could sleep on the sofa. This seemed like a good arrangement to the girl, so they made the deal. That night, when Julie and her children knelt down to say their prayers, they all thanked God for finding Mommy a job. And so Julie left to begin her new job at the Big Wheel Truck Stop. Even though times were rough, Julie thanked God that they had a roof over their heads, food to eat, clothes to keep them warm, and, most important, love in their hearts.

When the tires on her old truck began to leak, Julie would stop every evening on the way to work to fill the tires with air, and every morning before going home she would have to stop and do it again. One bleak fall morning Julie walked to her truck to go home, and to her complete surprise she found four tires in the backseat. She was absolutely elated. "New tires!" she screamed so loudly that everyone in the parking lot turned to look. There was no note, no nothing, just those big, beautiful, brand-new tires. Julie was sure that angels were watching over her.

Christmas was coming, and Julie knew there would be no money for toys for the kids. One day she found a can of red paint and started repairing and painting some old toys. Then she secretly hid them in the basement so that there would be something for Santa to deliver on Christmas morning. And every day when Julie finished her chores she would pray with all her heart that her children would have a Christmas to remember.

When Julie left work at six o'clock on Christmas morning, she hurried to her truck. She was hoping to arrive before the kids woke up so that she could carry the presents from the basement and place them under their small tree. It was still dark when she reached the truck and she couldn't see much, but there appeared to be some dark shadows in the truck. Or was that just a trick of the night? Something certainly looked different, but she couldn't tell what.

When Julie reached the truck, she peered into one of the side windows. Then her jaw dropped in amazement. Her old, battered truck was full to the top with boxes of all shapes and sizes. She quickly opened the driver's side door, scrambled inside, and knelt in the front facing the backseat. Reaching back, she pulled off the lid of the top box. Inside was a whole case of little blue jeans, sizes 2–10. She looked inside another box: it was full of shirts to go with the jeans. Then she peeked inside some of the other boxes: they held candy and nuts and bananas and bags of groceries. There was an enormous ham, canned vegetables, potatoes, and a whole bag of laundry supplies and cleaning items. And then, in the last box, she found three large toy trucks and one beautiful little doll.

Julie drove back through the empty streets as the sun slowly rose on the most amazing Christmas Day of her life. She breathed in a sigh of relief, knowing now for certain that God was answering her prayers. She sobbed uncontrollably with gratitude. When she stepped into her home, everyone was still asleep, so she carefully placed all the toys under their sparsely decorated little tree. When the children woke up, they found Julie with tears running down her cheeks. She couldn't stop crying. She told her children that God had answered her prayers and motioned them to open their presents. Julie watched and savored each smile and squeal of delight as her children opened all their presents. She vowed to never forget the joy on the faces of her children that precious Christmas morning. From that moment on Julie was sure that God listens, and she knew with certainty that there were angels hanging out at the Big Wheel Truck Stop that December.

There are angels surrounding each one of us right now, at this very moment. They live around the corner, work in your office, patrol your neighborhood, call you just to say hello, and are there to listen to you cry. They teach your children; they are your children. They pray for you and watch out for you, though you may never know it. And most of the time you see them every day without even recognizing them.

BELIEVING IN MIRACLES

The challenge for us is that when we feel most vulnerable and unsure, we are asked to open our hearts and let down the barriers that prevent us from feeling the love and support of the Universe. The third spiritual law asks us to trust that divine guidance is there for us. Even though this may seem like a difficult task if we've been hurt or betrayed, it is the only way we can heal our hearts and experience love again. We can break through the barriers we've built that prevent us from experiencing ourselves and each other only by letting go of our preconceived ideas about how life is and how our partners are.

Miracles can show up only when we are open to receiving them. If we are certain of who our partner is and of how he or she will react and behave in every situation, there is no room for that person to show up any differently. But if we let go and open up to the idea that at every moment each of us can change, we allow people and circumstances to show up differently. If you are attached to the belief that you can't make it on your own or that you won't have enough money to pay your bills, you are shutting yourself off from receiving a miracle, whether in the form of a job, a loan, or extra help from your partner.

FINDING SUPPORT

When we're ready, the Universe provides us with the support we need. It may come in the form of a book, a therapist, a group, a new friend, or a new idea. Once we cultivate our faith, we are divinely guided to the exact next thing we need.

Jill got married when she was twenty-one. At thirty-five she found out that her husband, Henry, was having an affair. Jill was the mother of three children, and as her husband seemed to lose interest in her, she focused on her children. They struggled to work it out for about a year, but no matter how Jill tried to patch things up, her marriage only seemed to get worse.

When Jill finally told Henry to move out, he immediately moved in with his girlfriend. Jill felt rejected and unloved. She waited at home for three weeks for their mutual friends to reach out and call, but no one did. She realized that she'd have to do something, for she was in desperate need of support. Every night after tucking her children into bed Jill prayed for a sign, something that would help her through this terrible time. She had faith that she would be led to support.

Then one morning, while reading the paper, she saw her sign. A meeting of a single parents' support group was scheduled for the next evening at a local synagogue. Jill asked her mother to baby-sit and went to her first meeting. She was surprised at the liveliness of everyone attending. Both the men and the women were warm and welcoming, and everyone began sharing their experiences with her. The group called themselves the Dumpees, which made Jill both laugh and cry, but she was relieved to have some humor back in her life. Jill became active in the group and after five weeks went on a date with one of the other members. She had a great time, and her date thought she was charming and even laughed at her jokes. She began to feel beautiful and desirable once again.

Jill made many new friends, and three years later, after being actively involved in her support group, she met David. They married, and David encouraged Jill to pursue her dream of going to law school. At age forty-three she passed the bar, and she is now a practicing attorney. Looking back, Jill wonders how she could ever have been married to her first husband. Faith and trust opened her eyes to the divine intervention that supported her in moving on with her life.

In the midst of our pain we must declare that even if everything around us falls apart—we become sick, we lose custody of our children, our friends desert us, or we run out of money—"God never gives us more than we can handle." Even though we may not see or feel God's love, it is always guiding and protecting us, and if we stay in this consciousness, we will prevail. When we are suffering and feeling all the turmoil of our separation, it is because we have allowed our consciousness to fall to the level where fear and limitation exist.

If in the midst of our pain we refuse to accept anything other than the reality of peace, love, and security, and we hold on to this reality as our truth, our consciousness will be purified and new thoughts will arise. These thoughts lift us up rather than pull us down. They offer hope and possibility rather than despair and hopelessness.

QUIETING YOUR MIND

Peace can exist only in a quiet mind. After my separation from Dan, I felt as if my life was spinning out of control. Struggling to make a living on my own, coping with being a single mother, and managing the day-to-day household chores were more than I could handle. I found myself constantly complaining about how chaotic my life was. It finally occurred to me that salvation would come only if I spent time each day going within. I made the decision to recommit myself to a daily meditation practice. One day while sitting quietly I saw that the chaos I had been complaining about was being fed by my own negative internal dialogue. Meditation became my tool for reclaiming my inner peace despite my outer circumstances.

The pain of divorce drives us deep into our negative internal dialogue, dredging up all our past grievances, judgments, hurts, and disappointments. The continuous chatter that incessantly fills our heads makes up the world that we live in and carves out the reality of our present and our future. Until we realize that our thoughts are nothing more than internal noise filled with fantasy and fear, we cannot transcend our suffering and find emotional balance.

When we meditate, we fall into the stillness that lives beyond our thoughts. The practice of meditation takes us beyond our conscious mind and into the quiet peace of divine guidance. When we meditate, we cease activity, fall still, and silently observe our thoughts and emotions. The goal of meditation is to reconnect with ourselves by disengaging from the automatic repetitive thoughts that bind us to the drama and pain of our divorce.

The practice of meditation is simple. Just sit quietly and comfortably, close your eyes, and begin by taking a few long, slow, deep breaths. Breathe consciously, putting all your attention on the movement and the sound of your breath. Feel your breath as it passes through the back of your throat and as it moves into your chest and abdomen. Continue putting your awareness on the inflow and outflow of your breath, and when your attention wanders to a thought, a feeling, or a sensation in your body, gently return your attention to your breathing. In the beginning you may be able to sit still for only five or ten minutes, but with practice you may find that you can enjoy thirty or forty minutes a day of sacred silence.

Another technique that you can use to find peace in the midst of chaos is what my friend and teacher Sarano Kelly calls "falling still." This practice asks you to take one or two minutes to fall still, to reconnect with your higher self so that you can be more aware of your actions and make better choices. Before getting on the phone to talk to your ex, before visiting the lawyer to discuss mediation, before picking the kids up from school, before paying the bills—anytime you find yourself feeling stress—take a moment to fall still.

You can have a taste of the practice of falling still right now by closing your eyes and taking five slow, deep breaths. Just imagine that you're falling into the still quiet place deep within you as you continue to breathe. Let all your thoughts, all your fears, all your worries—just for a moment—fall completely away. Allow them to melt into the earth.

Our inner peace is restored only when we learn to move beyond the ongoing dialogue that rattles around in our heads. If our minds are quiet, completely still, without thoughts, there are no problems, and no pain.

THE POWER OF PRAYER

Prayer raises our consciousness and heals our hearts. When our hearts are filled with hope, faith, and trust, we radiate a confidence that affects every area of our lives. Prayer is the tool that supports us in raising our consciousness to a spiritual level where our problems disappear. When we commit to practicing spiritual renewal, we work toward only one goal, and that goal is to purify our minds. Through prayer we rid ourselves of self-doubt and self-condemnation, and we make room for love, praise, and hope to permeate our consciousness. In the darkness of divorce prayer can be our refuge, providing us with the peace and clarity we so desperately need.

Emmett Fox tells us that we must stop thinking of the trouble, whatever it is. "The rule is to think about God, and if you are thinking about your difficulty, you are not thinking about God." You must actively and deliberately welcome God into your heart and into your life. You must have faith that God can and will take care of you and your family.

During the hardest times of my divorce I used prayer as a way to nourish my soul and bring me home to the comfort of God's love. When I opened my eyes in the morning, I would say a prayer asking God to do for me what I could not do for myself. I knew that if I could find relief from my negative emotions, I would have a day of peace, but if I could not find a way to transcend my negative thoughts and feelings, I would have another day of anger, frustration, and fear. Prayer became the medicine for my broken heart.

Whenever I feel anxious, depressed, scared, or angry, I continuously repeat an affirmation of God's love. I pray for acceptance and the wisdom to make the right choices. The purpose of prayer is to shift our consciousness, and when we use prayer as a spiritual treatment, it eliminates our fear and suffering and replaces it with faith and trust.

If you ask the Universe to be your partner and guide you on the path to wholeness, it will oblige. When you are in pain, it so easy to fall into the self-defeating pattern of feeling sorry for yourself. You may even think that you deserve to feel sorry for yourself, but when you pray, you are lifted out of your suffering and into the experience of faith and divine intervention.

Asking for divine guidance makes possible the experience of universal partnership. The most difficult step for most people is to move God from a concept in their head to an experience in their heart. Through meditation, rituals, and dedicated prayer work, we can be led to a shift in consciousness, the first step to creating an extraordinary life.

HEALING ACTION STEPS

1. Create a place in your home for an altar. An altar reminds you that you're not alone. It is your sacred space where you can pray, meditate, journal, cry, or contemplate your life. You'll want to deem it a "holy place" and treat it as such. It can be in your bedroom or any other area of your home. An altar is generally created over time by collecting items that inspire you and bring forth images of love and compassion. On my altar I have pictures of many holy saints. I keep a picture of my son and all the other family members I love. You may also want to include a picture of yourself as a child and as a grownup. The picture should be from a time when you felt happy or content. You can put down a beautiful scarf or other fabric as the foundation of your altar. Decorate it with pictures, candles, and any other items that give you comfort. Include any kind of symbol of your faith. You may want to add a Bible or prayer book. If you don't have any prayer books that you like, create your own prayer, print it on some special paper, and include it on your altar. Your altar will provide you with a serene place to pray, meditate, and find inner comfort.

2. Set aside some time each day for meditation. Find a comfortable space in your home where you are not likely to be disturbed. Just sit comfortably and begin watching your breath. As you breathe in,

say to yourself, *I am loved,* and as you breathe out, say, *I am lovable.* Breathe in *I am healed,* and breathe out *I am whole.* Start out doing this for ten minutes a day and gradually increase the length of time you spend in silence.

3. Select a prayer to use as your divorce prayer. Use it with the intention of healing your heart. If you don't know a prayer, you can either use one of the prayers that I share here or search through a Bible or a prayer book. I highly recommend Marianne Williamson's bestselling book *Illuminata.* You can also get quiet and write your own prayer. Once you have selected your prayer and written it down, go to your altar, get comfortable standing, sitting, or kneeling, and then repeat your prayer out loud or to yourself at least five times. End your prayer by saying, "Thank you, God, for listening. I know my prayer is being answered even as we speak."

THE LAW OF

RESPONSIBILITY

Chapter Five

EMOTIONAL RESPONSIBILITY

The only devils in the world are those running around in our hearts. That is where the battle should be fought.

MAHATMA GANDHI

The Law of Responsibility tells us that once we have asked God to come into our lives and guide us, we will begin to heal. With the help and support of our Divine Protector, we can embark on the journey to explore our inner world. With God by our side, we gain the strength we need to take ownership of our emotional baggage. We can take ownership only when we realize that we played an equal role in the breakdown of our marriage. Although we may not feel ready to accept this task, now is the time to turn the focus back to ourselves and to stop blaming others for being the source of our suffering.

When you are separating from your partner, you may be tempted to focus on his or her wrongdoings or shortcomings. You point your finger at your ex-spouse because you may fear that if you focus on yourself, you will sink into depression and regret. But the only way to heal is to look within. Taking total responsibility for your own life requires that you face your fear. You must look deeply into yourself and see your divorce not as the cause of your problems but as a symptom of all your unhealed emotional issues. You must acknowledge that your pain and problems are rooted deep within yourself. Even though taking responsibility may seem like a monumental task at this moment, it is your only alternative. The Law of Responsibility is your guide to the entranceway to emotional freedom.

When Dan and I were separating, I was resentful and angry at him for putting me through so much unnecessary pain. I was convinced that if only he would do what I wanted him to do, our problems would go away. I was living under the illusion that my pain had nothing to do with me and everything to do with Dan. I was sure that if only he would fix himself, I would be okay. I began listing all the changes that I thought would make Dan the person I wanted him to be. My list looked like this:

Dan needs to go to therapy and work on his unresolved emotions.

Dan needs to let go of control and allow me to be his teacher.

Dan needs to stop lying about what's really going on in our marriage.

Dan needs to stop blaming me for our problems.

After studying my list, it occurred to me that the prescription I was writing for Dan was the exact medicine I needed to heal myself. So I substituted my own name for Dan's, and then my list looked like this:

I need to go to therapy and work on my unresolved emotions.

I need to let go of control and allow Dan to be my teacher.

I need to stop lying about what's really going on in our marriage.

I need to stop blaming Dan for our problems.

Although it angered me to no end, I had to admit that I had a lot of unresolved emotions that needed to be healed. Looking beyond my defenses, I could see that I had fought to control our lives, because I believed that I "knew better." I continually resisted Dan's guidance in any way. It was a little more difficult for me to see how many lies I had told because I had convinced myself that withholding the truth isn't a lie. And, of course, it was easy to see that I always had my finger pointed at Dan, blaming him for everything that wasn't working in our lives. I knew that to heal myself I had to stop blaming Dan and own up to being an equal partner in the dissolution of our marriage.

Awareness of our feelings is fundamental to healing our hearts. Our toxic emotions linger on until we learn the lessons they are trying to teach us. In the beginning of my separation from Dan, my feelings were out of control. One minute I was happy, and the next minute I was angry. I'd burst into tears while changing a diaper or have an anxiety attack while putting away the dishes. There was no rhyme or reason to these feelings; they just randomly surfaced. But then a friend kindly pointed out that all these emotions were mine, living inside of me. That day I stopped blaming Dan and took ownership of all my negative feelings.

Every time I experienced one of these unwanted feelings I would sit down and close my eyes. Then I would identify exactly what I was feeling at that moment. If I felt sad, I would ask myself, *What am I sad about? Is it the loss of a sexual partner? Is it the loss of my son's father being at home? Is it a loss of security? Is it the death of a dream?* Identifying and acknowledging the source of my sadness was the beginning of my healing.

Often I would think I was sad about not having Dan to sleep with, but when I got quiet and did some deep breathing, I would realize that I was sad about being so far away from my family. This is why it's so important to close our eyes and go within to ask, because often our head tells us one thing and our heart tells us something else. After I found and named the source of my sadness, I would take out my divorce journal and begin free-writing, jotting down whatever thoughts or feelings I was experiencing at the moment. Without thinking about what or why I was writing, I would just allow myself to write, to purge onto the paper. In one of my divorce journals I wrote:

Today I woke up in a well of emptiness. Feeling totally disconnected I got out of bed and tried to pretend that I was okay. But truth be told I'm not. I'm so scared, frightened of the rest of my life. Where will I go and what will I do? Who will be there to protect and take care of me? Finally, I thought this part of my life was taken care of, my loneliness gone. But here I am again, back further than when my marriage began. Now I have more to worry about, another mouth to feed, another soul to care for. I'm drowning in a sea of sadness. Everywhere I look I see another obstacle, another roadblock.

When I finished journaling, I would close my eyes and ask God to please help me heal. Then I would try to remember other times in my life when I had experienced that feeling. Inevitably those other times floated into my consciousness. Often these memories would bring up more pain and more sadness. When that happened, I allowed myself to breathe deeply into my pain and acknowledge these old feelings. Then I would take out my journal again and write about my other experiences that were linked to this same pain. When I finished, I would take some slow, deep breaths, putting all my awareness on the feeling. Then I would pray silently for my heart to be healed. What I realized was that I couldn't heal, I couldn't feel better, until I had "owned" my feelings and taken responsibility for both my actions and my nonactions.

STEPPING INTO THE STORM

Taking ownership of our emotions is the only way to take back our power and regain control of our lives. We can't heal what we can't feel. Stepping into the storm of our turbulent emotions represents a sacred and significant time in our lives. It is during this time that we get to know our deepest selves. Standing in the storm of our emotions allows us to feel the depth of our own woundedness and the agony of our broken hearts. It exposes our internal conflicts and challenges all that we believe about ourselves.

Divorce is one of the darkest times in most people's lives. It's a time when we question everyone and everything. Separating from our partners affects every aspect of our lives and rocks the foundation of our entire being. Unexpectedly, the kindest woman may become a raging bull, or the most generous man may start lying and hiding his money. Good mothers and fathers suddenly break all the rules, coming late for visits with their children and bad-mouthing their ex in front of innocent ears. The best-intentioned people may become vengeful and willing to give everything up to lawyers rather than succumb to their enemy's wishes. All of this insanity is a symptom of our unhealed emotional wounds. Our anger, bitterness, grief, fear, guilt, and shame drive us to behaviors that sabotage our happiness. Now is the time to examine our thoughts, beliefs, and judgments while taking a courageous leap into the core of our pain.

Marc was in the middle of separating from his wife of seven years when he attended the Shadow Process. He appeared defensive and angry, but when I asked him to identify his painful emotions, he said he wasn't aware of any. I asked Marc why his marriage was ending, and he told me that his wife had ended it after finding out that he had been seeing another woman. I then had Marc close his eyes and ask himself, "What kind of person would cheat on his wife?" The word that popped into his mind and out of his mouth was *betrayer.* Then I asked him how he felt when I said the words, "Marc, you are a betrayer." Immediately he opened his eyes and shouted, "But I'm *not* a betrayer. I had to find someone to have sex with because my wife didn't want to!" I asked Marc whether he thought it was fair to blame his wife for his extramarital affairs, and he just sat there, shaking his head in shame. Then Marc quietly confessed that he had always hated the word *betrayer,* because that was the same label he had stamped on his cheating father.

I encouraged Marc to stay with the process, explaining to him that in order to heal and make peace with what he had done he would need to embrace what it felt like to be a betrayer. I asked Marc to repeat after me: "I am a betrayer. I am a betrayer. I am a betrayer." After repeating this twenty or thirty times, Marc finally was in the presence of the agony and the pain he felt around betraying his wife. He was overcome with guilt, hurt, shame, and the sadness that he had turned into his father, the one person he never wanted to be.

SPIRITUAL DIVORCE

Marc had to breathe, cry, and stay with his emotions before he could finally accept and embrace this deep emotional wound. He had blamed his wife for her lack of sexual drive for so long that he had fooled himself into believing that he had a right to cheat on her. After he was able to be with these feelings—his anger, his sadness, his loss, and his grief—he stood in the humility and vulnerability of his own imperfections. Only then could he feel remorse and grief over his actions.

By stepping into the storm of his emotions, Marc was able to discover the true feelings that lay beneath his defensiveness. By allowing his pain to come to the surface, he opened up the space for new emotions to arise. After many hours of contemplation, Marc decided that he would finally have to face the pain of his childhood and make peace with the part of him that was so much like his father. But now he was standing in a calm, compassionate place where he could make the changes necessary without hurting himself or his wife. As soon as Marc stepped into the truth of his emotional pain, he stopped pointing his finger at his wife and took complete and total responsibility for his actions and the pain he had caused.

To dissolve the conflicted energies that lie at the root of our pain we must feel them and acknowledge what we have felt or done without resistance or judgment. As we pass through each emotion, which is energy in motion, we will experience a deep and quiet inner peace. Owning our feelings allows us to drop deeper into the stillness that lies within us. In this stillness we can begin to see the light in our darkness and start to make choices that will heal us rather than defeat us.

ARE YOU WILLING TO HEAL?

Our toxic emotions—our anger, resentment, jealousy, guilt, and shame—fester inside of us, calling for our attention. These emotions cannot be healed without acknowledgment, love, and compassion. Only then do they lose their power over us. When left unattended, they leave us feeling fearful, tired, and sick. For many, our withheld anger turns to depression, leaving us paralyzed, unable to move forward with our lives. Often what gets in the way of healing toxic emotions is a deep sense of resignation, a sense of failure, a feeling of powerlessness, of having no choice or control over our emotional well-being. Making a commitment to let go of our sour emotions is a declaration to the Universe that we are ready to take responsibility for our lives.

Some people insist on holding on to their emotional poison and won't do anything about it. Instead of admitting that they *won't* do something, they say, "I can't." But "I can't" is a lie—it's an irresponsible way of saying, "I won't." To take responsibility is to acknowledge, "I did this." Even if I can't see how I did it, or why I did it, the very fact that this problem is in my life tells me that I have participated in its creation.

At one of my recent seminars I met Jody, a young woman who was suffering from the breakup of her relationship. Before the seminar even began, Jody told everyone who would listen that she wasn't going to get anything out of the weekend, that the seminar wasn't going to help her. Jody had convinced herself that her pain was bigger than everyone else's, and different. Whenever I asked everyone to close their eyes to do an exercise, Jody would sit there with her eyes open. During the breaks, when all the other participants were trying to do the homework, Jody was busy making small talk with anyone who would listen.

By the end of the third day, when everyone else was joyously sharing their insights and love, Jody was sulking in her chair. When I walked over to her at the end to find out how she was doing, she just looked at me and said, "I told you I wasn't going to get it!" It wasn't that Jody couldn't get it, rather that she wouldn't take responsibility for her own healing process and refused to do the work that was necessary for her to heal. Jody was waiting for it to happen to her.

The first step in taking responsibility for healing your pain is to acknowledge that it is *your* pain. The second step is to make the decision to give it up. You can do it! You must ask yourself, *Do I want to hold on to this pain? Do I want to walk around for another week, month,*

year, or even a lifetime with the bitterness of my past etched on my face?
Am I willing to change?

It's imperative to understand that in order for an emotion to be triggered with a high level if intensity it has to be linked to another wound within you. So even though there are many ways to avoid dealing with your feelings, a lot of evidence says that at some time in your life, if not properly dealt with, the feeling will surface again. It will rear its ugly little head in another time of great distress. This is the time to really understand the saying "You can run, but you can't hide."

IDENTIFYING OUR FEELINGS

Identifying our feelings—both positive and negative—and developing an understanding of our emotional world provides us with new ways of coping with our lives. To understand the full range of human emotions all we have to do is spend a few hours with a baby. One minute the baby will be smiling, rolling around in a blanket of joy, and a second later that same blissful baby will be screaming like a banshee. Then, as quickly as that anger appeared, it will disappear, leaving the child in yet another emotional state.

Babies innocently show us the full range of emotion, both positive and negative. They display the flexible and transformative nature of our feelings. They show us the quietness of deep peace and the volatility of anger. As children, we accept all of our feelings without judgment. We understand that the outer expression of our emotions is the way we express our needs and wants. And it's not until we're told that it's not okay to cry, to be quiet, to stop that screaming that our full range of emotions begins to shut down.

The negative feedback from our elders begins the process of making our feelings wrong. Seeing how our emotions trigger bad or good responses in the people we love has us hide our true feelings and cover up our authentic expression. We make significant conclusions that often last our entire lives when we decide what emotions are safe to express and which ones are best left hidden away. Soon we find ourselves immersed in a mélange of feelings, some of them unrecognizable to us.

For many people the uncontrollable swell of negative emotions brought forth by their separation is a new experience. I'm often told by clients who are in the midst of divorce, "I didn't know I could ever get so angry," or, "I never thought I could hate someone so much." Whether it's anger, jealousy, hate, shame, embarrassment, or guilt, these feelings need to be brought to the surface and healed. Most people just try to figure out ways to hide, get rid of, or medicate their unwelcome emotions rather than exploring and discovering the root of their existence.

RELEASING TOXIC EMOTIONS

Imagine holding a soda bottle that has been shaken up. If you take the cap off fast, the soda explodes and squirts out everywhere, leaving you with a huge mess. But if you take that same shaken bottle, hold it over a sink, and slowly loosen the cap, instead of making a huge mess you'll be able to contain and settle down the contents of the bottle.

Similarly, our emotions need a safe container for healing. In times of distress, when our feelings are shaken up, they seek release. They search and find ways to come out in order to release some of the internal pressure. If we're filled with anger, we find things in the outside world to be angry at. If we're sad and depressed, we either create trauma around ourselves, so as to have excuses for our bad feelings, or focus on the negative aspects of others. Unless we look within and take responsibility for our own part in our divorce, we will continually seek an outside cause for our feelings. That's why it's so important to go within to heal our wounds, to take the time to find a safe way to release what's inside us. In the Sermon on the Mount, Jesus said, "If you bring forth what is within you, what is within you will save you. If you do not bring forth what is within you, what is within you will destroy you."

Our pain is coded with messages that, when understood, propel us to attain new states of awareness. Unhappiness, anxiety, fear, and depression are the consequences of not dealing with our painful emotions. Instead of looking at our uncomfortable feelings as something to dispose of, we must try to see them for what they are—guides leading us inside so that we can heal ourselves at the deepest levels. It is only through accepting exactly how we feel in this moment, even if it's angry and hateful, that we can heal our toxic emotions. When we take the time to listen to the feelings that live within us, we begin to transform our sadness into joy, our anger into compassion, our fear into faith, and our pain into pleasure.

EXTERNALIZING YOUR EMOTIONS

Sherri is thirty-eight years old, childless, and divorced for four years. She has been waiting to meet the man of her dreams and start a family. For six months Sherri believed that she had finally found that man in Josh. Sherri and Josh met through mutual friends, were from the same ethnic background, and shared many of the same beliefs about religion and family. Sherri was beside herself with joy thinking that the man of her dreams had finally arrived. Then one day Josh stopped calling. Without a word there were no more phone calls, no more e-mails. When Sherri reached out and called Josh, her calls went unanswered. Sherri was devastated and lapsed into a severe depression.

When Sherri arrived at my door, I saw a beautiful young woman with very sad eyes. Something inside her had died, and it showed all over her face. We began talking, and Sherri recounted all the events that had led up to her visit. She had been married for ten years to Allen, a man who was an alcoholic and verbally abusive. Sherri went through what she believed were some of their issues, and when I asked how it ended, she told me that one day Allen got mad at her and just stopped speaking to her. For almost a year they lived together in the same house and he never said one word to her. When she finally decided to leave him, she didn't want anything from him, so she departed with just her divorce papers. They haven't spoken since.

Sherri and I sat in silence for a long time. And then she began to cry as she told me another story, this time about her father. When Sherri was in high school, she went out one night with her friends. She had always had a curfew of 10:00 P.M., but that night, for whatever reason, Sherri decided to stay out later. When she arrived home at midnight, her father was sitting in their dark living room waiting for her. In his fury Sherri's father called her every bad name he could think of. Then he stood up and told her that he was disowning her as his daughter, and from that moment on Sherri's father refused to utter one word to her for almost six months.

The story seemed almost unbelievable. Three of the most important men in her life just stopped speaking to her. When I asked Sherri what she learned from these situations, she didn't have an answer. She just looked at me with a blank stare on her face. With great distress, she admitted that she had never even made the connection. In Sherri's mind each man represented very different issues.

Sherri and I set out to expose all the toxic emotions that were within her. I reaffirmed that there are indeed no accidents, and that until she learned from these incidents and explored the pain she was feeling, it would probably continue. I asked Sherri to close her eyes and do some breathing. I wanted her to get in touch with another feeling besides the sadness. It took us two weeks, but in the second week, when Sherri was going inside and asking herself what she felt besides sadness, she finally connected with her anger. Suddenly this rather meek, quiet woman was experiencing some very volatile emotions. All the anger and rage that she had denied so long ago finally came out. First it was directed at her father; by week four it had moved to her first husband, and in the fifth week she was able to express her anger toward Josh. Instead of blaming herself and feeling depressed, she was able to speak and write about a feeling that had been deeply buried within her for many years.

I assigned Sherri the task of finding a way to externalize her anger in a safe way. Anger had never been an acceptable emotion for the women in her family, so the thought of freely expressing herself was terrifying. She decided that she would try "batting." In the beginning she would whack a few pillows for a couple of minutes and then stop. I suggested that Sherri go to the local music store, buy the meanest, nastiest Nine Inch Nails CD she could find, and put it on while doing her daily practice of anger release. It took a while, but one day Sherri finally gave herself permission just to let go. And out came years of anger, rage, and pain. She continued for a couple of months, and the more she released her stored emotions in a safe way, the better she began to feel.

I wanted Sherri to find the lesson in her pain. One day she came to see me and said, "You'll never believe this, but last week, when I left your house, I was trying to figure out what all these men were trying to teach me, and what came to me was that they were all trying to teach me to love myself."

She told me that she had always been mean to herself and that it wasn't until she walked out of my house that day and got in her car that she realized just how very mean she had been. That day, when she got behind the wheel, she did the same thing she had always done. She adjusted the rearview mirror so that she could see herself, she looked at her face, and then she heard these words in her head: *You're so ugly. Why would anyone love you? Go home and put on some makeup.* Sherri began to cry, overwhelmed by the meanness of her internal voice. In a moment of grace Sherri observed that the outer world was reflecting the way she mistreated herself. Finally she could see that the men in her life who had beaten up on her were trying to show her that she was beating up on herself.

If you externalize your emotions in healthy ways, you won't have to beat up on yourself or your partner. Any emotion that is denied, hidden, or suppressed takes on a life of its own, undermining your feelings of inner worthiness and upsetting your natural state of peace. Imagine taking a sip of sour milk and instead of spitting it out you swallow it. Now your stomach and everything in it is contaminated with this sour taste and you feel sick. This is what it's like when we swallow our feelings. They fester inside us, leaving us angry, frustrated, nervous, weak, and tired. It's important to understand that spitting up your sour milk on your partner is not the answer, that this only creates more toxicity. But there are ways to release your negative feelings without hurting anyone else.

In the middle of my divorce, Dan often said things over the phone that would trigger my anger. I knew that screaming at him only made things worse, so I'd take a deep breath and tell him I'd have to call him back. After hanging up the phone, I would grab a plastic baseball bat, go into the closet, and beat on some pillows. For a couple of months I just left the pillow and bat in my closet because I constantly found myself so full of rage and resentment that I could barely think about anything else. After I finished screaming and raging at the pillow, I always felt a release. A calmness would surround me, and I could think more clearly. Then I would journal and pray, asking God to support me in my effort to heal without hurting Dan or taking out my anger on Beau. Then, feeling calm, I would pick up the phone and call Dan back to resume our conversation.

Our toxic emotions can have devastating effects on others, leaving wounds that may last a lifetime. If we learn healthy ways to release our emotions, we can save ourselves and others from the negative impact of our emotional outbursts.

Recently I heard a story about a little boy named Jimmy who had a bad temper. One day Jimmy's father gives him a bag of nails and tells him that every time he loses his temper he has to hammer a nail into the back of the fence. By the end of the first day Jimmy has driven twenty nails into the fence. Over the next few weeks, as Jimmy learns to control his anger, the number of nails he has to hammer into the fence each day gradually dwindles. Jimmy discovers that it is easier to hold his temper than to drive those nails into the fence. Finally the day comes when Jimmy doesn't lose his temper at all. Excited, Jimmy tells his father about it, and his dad suggests that Jimmy now pull out one nail for each day he is able to hold his temper.

The days pass, and Jimmy is finally able to tell his father that all the nails are gone. His dad takes him by the hand and leads him to the fence. He says, "You have done well, my son, but look at the holes in the fence. The fence will never be the same. When you say things in anger, they leave a scar just like this one. You can put a knife in a man and draw it out. It won't matter how many times you say, 'I'm sorry'; the wound is still there."

Verbal abuse often leaves wounds as severe as those caused by physical abuse. To ensure that we don't leave holes in our partners or our children we must bring light to our hidden darkness. Once we bring awareness to our open wounds, we begin to have control over our emotional world. We can then make a conscious choice to deal with our emotions in healthy ways instead of being sucked into the darkness of hurting others.

It takes only a little light to dispel our dark feelings, but it is in our darkness that we find our light. Beyond our anger, resentment, and pain is a sea of love so great and so vast that it can wash away any wound. Light a candle or shine a light in a dark room, and you will witness the power of light and how quickly the dark disappears.

No one else can release your toxic emotions; no one can save you from the ill effects of swallowing quart after quart of spoiled milk. You are the only one who can make that decision. You and the people who care the most about you are the ones who will ultimately be hurt if you don't assume responsibility for your feelings, regardless of who did what to whom. When you become accountable for ridding yourself of all your sour milk, you can move on with your life.

RELATIONSHIP INVENTORY

Taking responsibility that this is your life, your emotions, and your negative feelings creates an internal movement that supports you in becoming free from your pain and from repeating it in the future. As long as you continue to blame someone else, you're stuck in the illusion that you are powerless over your condition. Until you take total responsibility for the circumstances you find yourself in, you remain powerless to change them. Once you embrace your own part in your circumstances, you can begin to face and embrace what is within you.

We embark on this journey by taking an inventory of our relationship. Being rigorously honest about our actions, behaviors, and shortcomings allows us to see clearly how we participated in the breakdown of our partnership. Any trace of denial or self-protection keeps us stuck blaming others and unable to move forward with our lives. Here is Sherri's relationship inventory as an example:

1. I didn't care about my spouse's needs.
2. I spent more money than he wanted me to.
3. I made plans with my family and friends and discouraged him from doing the same.
4. I kept him on a tight leash, monitoring his whereabouts.
5. I criticized his way of dressing.
6. I didn't want to have sex.
7. I blamed him for my unhappiness.
8. I ignored my own values to get him to love me.
9. I didn't deal with my childhood wounds and took out my anger on him.
10. I complained about all the things he didn't do.

Your toxic emotions need understanding and compassion. Only by owning your feelings do you gain the power to change them. As long as you are blaming others for how you feel, you are condemned to a life of suffering. At this moment you may feel trapped, powerless to confront your emotions. But all you need to do is to be patient and willing to love all that you have feared. Then you will be blessed with the gift of peace and serenity.

HEALING ACTION STEPS

1. Close your eyes and take three slow, deep breaths. Begin by asking yourself, *What am I feeling at this moment?* After you've given

the emotion a name, give yourself permission to feel whatever it is you're feeling. When you're ready, put all your attention on the feeling and slowly breathe deeply into the energy of this emotion. Notice the judgments you make about this feeling and write them down. If it's anger you're feeling, you might write, "I hate my anger because my mother was angry," or, "Everyone told me that only stupid people get angry, so I'm embarrassed when I get angry." After you've written down your judgments, allow yourself to give some outer expression to the feeling, like yelling as loud as you can in your car or punching a pillow. (One of the biggest lies I've ever heard is that catharsis doesn't work. It may not work for everyone, but it certainly works for everyone I've ever done it with.) Then express your feeling to God and yourself. You might enlist a friend to listen, without judgment, as you talk about your feeling.

2. In your divorce journal—for your eyes only—write an anger letter to your partner, expressing to him or her all your rage, anger, disdain, resentment, disappointment, and sadness. The purpose is to purge the toxic emotions stored inside you, so don't withhold anything. If you're afraid this letter might be discovered, write it and then burn it, but give yourself full permission to discharge your toxic emotions once and for all.

3. Make a list of all the resentments you are holding against your partner. Then list all the grievances you are holding against other people.

4. Take a relationship inventory and make a list of all the behaviors and actions that didn't work in your marriage. Include both what you did and what you didn't do.

Chapter Six

TO THINE OWN SELF BE TRUE

*Every human being is a mirror through which
God longs to see himself.*

DR. ROBERT SVOBODA

The Law of Responsibility supports us in recognizing that we have chosen the perfect partner to teach us the perfect lessons. Discovering and coming to terms with the similarities between our partner and ourselves gives us valuable information that is vital to our healing. Only through becoming intimate with each and every aspect of ourselves can we make peace with our partner and take complete responsibility for our lives.

While going through divorce, we expend huge amounts of energy differentiating ourselves from our partner in an effort to protect our self-image. Our internal radar continuously searches out all the ways in which we are different from or superior to the one who has threatened our emotional and physical security. We point our fingers in blame, distancing ourselves from the spouse we once loved. We may even convince ourselves that we do not share the traits we find so unbearable in our partner.

If we are going to take responsibility for our part in our divorce drama, we must begin to acknowledge the similarities between ourselves and our spouse. In the midst of divorce, when we are breaking our vows and our commitment to partnership, it's natural to focus on our differences.

When Dan and I first separated, I was sure that we were very different people. My belief at the time was that I was the healthy, more evolved partner, and that Dan was the unhealthy, unconscious half of our union. Even though deep down I understood that we pick partners with the same level of woundedness as our own, a part of me was trying desperately to deny this piece of information. I knew that my job was to find and reclaim the unconscious, unhealthy aspects of myself, but all I could see were Dan's shortcomings.

For weeks I tried looking at my life through clear eyes. Then one day, while I was pointing my finger at Dan and blaming him for my pain, I realized that only the unhealthy, unconscious part of me would blame someone else for my feelings. I saw that from the day we got married I had been blaming Dan for my circumstances. While a neat excuse, this explanation had the unfortunate downside of being a lie. And living a lie wasn't going to make me feel better. I had to admit that I had fallen into the trap of making Dan the bad guy and claiming the "good person" label for myself.

The universal language of divorce sounds like this: "I'm not like my husband," and, "My wife and I are two very different people." But I ask you to consider this: maybe you are more like your husband or wife than you've imagined. Maybe all the qualities that initially attracted you to your partner—and all the qualities that now repel you—are simply hidden aspects of yourself. And maybe your partner has in fact been the perfect mirror, enabling you to discover and heal those aspects of yourself that you have long judged or forgotten.

THE MYTH OF SEPARATISM

Most of us were raised to believe that we are separate and different from one another, and that there are good people and bad people. We were told that the bad people have qualities, traits, and behaviors that the good people don't have. Many of us have dedicated a large portion of our lives to getting rid of the bad qualities we've discovered in ourselves. But what if this way of perceiving the Universe and ourselves is no longer true? What if there aren't really any "bad people" qualities?

If we continue to believe that we are separate and that the good people are different from the bad, we will be doomed to a life of victimization, separation, and isolation. In the world of separatism, our egos must work hard to construct a persona that is better than or different from everyone around us. This persona is our social mask, the face we show the world. Most of us forget that it's just a persona and come to believe that our mask is who we really are. In the separatist worldview, the last thing you want to discover is that you have imperfections as bad as everyone else's, and it's especially bad news to discover this in the midst of a divorce. It is the nightmare of the ego to discover that at our core every one of us is created equal.

But don't you ever wonder how you found someone so unlike yourself? Do you ever ask yourself how you could have ever fallen in love with someone who would do this to you? Someone who pushes every button? Don't you ever wonder why the person you were married to can't see what you see, hear what you hear, or feel how you feel?

Almost everyone going through the process of divorce will tell you things about their partner that they can't tolerate. Everyone has a list of these unbearable qualities. We must understand, however, that all aspects of ourselves are vital to the integrity of the whole and that God doesn't make any spare parts. Carl Jung said, "I'd rather be whole than good." To be a whole person we need access to all of ourselves—the good and the bad. To be a whole human being is to be happy, sensitive, and content *and* sad, selfish, and angry. If we own only half of ourselves, the good part, but deny the other half, we're left feeling incomplete, as though we are not enough. We experience a gnawing feeling that something is wrong here.

I began to understand this concept while driving in my car listening to a taped lecture by Dr. Deepak Chopra. He explained that the

SPIRITUAL DIVORCE

Universe is holographic, meaning that the whole of the Universe is contained within every part. Although we tend to focus on our differences, human beings are fundamentally very much the same. The holographic model reveals that each of us is a microcosm of the macrocosm. It teaches us that beneath the surface of every human is a blueprint for all of mankind. To illustrate this point he shared a quote from an ancient text: "You are not in the world; the world is within you."

Though I didn't understand intellectually how this could possibly be true, these words sparked a deep inner knowing within me. And I knew I had just received a vital piece of information that would support me in my own spiritual awakening.

For months I pondered how the world and all its diversity could live inside of me. I even played a little game with myself. As I walked around San Francisco, I would look at people and say to myself, *You are within me.* It was easy to accept this idea when I liked the people I was observing. When I saw someone being generous, I would think to myself, *I am generous.* When I saw someone showing kindness, I was open to accepting that person as a part of me. But when I judged someone I saw as nasty, jealous, or controlling, I would think to myself, *Thank God I am not like that. I would never do that.*

Then one day, as I was riding the train to school, a woman across the aisle started screaming at her child. I was very upset by her outburst and thought to myself, *What an awful person.* I decided she was a bad mother who never should have had a child. Then a little voice in my head whispered, *If your child had just spilled chocolate milk all over your white suit on the way to work, you would be screaming like a banshee.*

I began to see that it wasn't the person who lived inside of me, but rather the qualities I saw the person displaying. I had thought of the screaming woman as impatient, disrespectful, and angry. Although I didn't have a child at the time, I could certainly see other places in my own life where I had been impatient, disrespectful, and angry. This is when I understood that every quality that exists on the planet exists within me. And even though I might not be expressing that trait at the same moment under the same circumstances, I would probably display some version of the same behavior in another time and place. This awareness was the key to taking responsibility for my life.

When you understand the profound design of the Universe, you can see that you contain everything you see in others. Then in an instant your entire world will alter. You will discover how all that you see and conceive is a reflection of your inner world. You understand why you can love someone one minute and hate him or her the next. You know why other people can say or do things that push your buttons and why these buttons are so charged with emotion.

To be whole we need access to all of ourselves. If we are brave and step into the reality that the world is within us, we can embrace the totality of what it means to be a human being. Expanding our consciousness to hold the enormity of the world within allows us to feel the strength, power, and balance of our humanity. It supports us in stepping out of judgment and separateness and into a knowing compassion. The moment I understood this I was no longer a victim of Dan's behavior. I could see that Dan was only reflecting a part of myself that I did not accept.

EMOTIONAL WHOLENESS

There are no qualities inside of us that don't have a purpose somewhere or at some time. We have fear so that we will know when we need to protect ourselves. Fear tells us when it's not safe to walk down a dark street or when to lock our doors. We have anger so that we will know when someone has violated us or crossed our boundaries. Our sadness enables us to feel the pain of loss; otherwise, how would we know that we miss someone or something? How would we measure the importance of people or things? How else would we recognize our disappointments? Joy tells us that our souls are being nourished, while discontent tells us that something is missing from our lives. I love my laziness, which gives me permission to cuddle up and take naps, but for someone else laziness may be a source of deep shame. There is no light without darkness because you wouldn't know it as light. We need the contrast so that we can distinguish and see the light.

You wouldn't know good without knowing bad. You would never recognize selfless if you hadn't experienced selfish. How would you be able to see humility if you had never known arrogance? It all serves a purpose, and maybe a little arrogance is just what you need to know that you deserve to have it all. We are all courageous and fearful, caring and careless, honest and deceitful. We are all powerful, compassionate, and creative as well as angry, lustful, and weak. Every quality we possess has its polar opposite close by waiting to come into balance. Emotional wholeness is the acknowledgment and integration of all our qualities.

In my quest to find emotional balance I had to look at how I had differentiated myself from Dan. When I was attached to seeing myself as the conscious member of our relationship, it blinded me to my unconscious behaviors. I couldn't take responsibility for co-creating the problems in our marriage because I was seeing only part of myself. By taking responsibility for my actions, I could see that I needed to embrace all of myself, and that my unconscious half was not wrong or bad but rather a necessary part of the whole.

When I was pointing my finger in blame, I was left feeling powerless. By owning and embracing my unconscious actions, I was able to bring myself back into balance and take responsibility for my part in the breakdown of our marriage. The moment I claimed responsibility for my circumstances the doomed feeling of powerlessness lifted. And instead of feeling angry and resentful, I was able to see Dan as the caring, sensitive man he is.

Understanding that everything we love and everything we hate are simply mirrors of our internal self enables us to stop projecting the unwanted and disowned aspects of ourselves onto our partner. Pointing our fingers and blaming others robs us of our right to health and wholeness. It keeps us stuck in the past, perpetuating the myth that we are victims of other people's behavior.

Take a deep breath and imagine that everyone who walks by you in the street and everyone you see or read about in the news is a reflection of some part of you. Consider for a moment that every quality you have ever admired in a teacher, lover, or friend, and every trait you've ever despised in your worst enemies, all exist inside of you. Within you are thousands of qualities, some lying dormant, some hidden out of sight. Some are active and some are inactive. All that you love about others and all that you hate about others are aspects that belong to you. The fact is that you wouldn't be able to recognize certain qualities in others if you didn't possess them yourself.

THE MIRROR OF RELATIONSHIP

We are designed with the great ability to observe everyone around us. Unless we are blind, our eyes enable us to see all of those who cross our path. We can walk into a room with a hundred people and look at them all. We can look around and observe each and every person; we can see what we like and what we dislike. But there will always be one person in the room that you can't see—that person is yourself. Unless you're standing in front of a mirror, you can't bring yourself into your own field of vision.

But our psyches trick us into believing that we can indeed see ourselves. Most of us would say, "I am the one who knows myself best." But how can we know ourselves if we can't even fully see ourselves? The answer to this question is simple: we can know ourselves through our God-given mirrors. I am your mirror, and you are mine. We are created perfectly. Since we can't see ourselves by ourselves, we were created with the reflective device of being able to see ourselves in each other. I can see myself every time I look at you. The outer world is my mirror, and when I see your kindness, I am able to view my own kindness. If I look at you and see your greed, I am seeing my own greed. And if I look at you and see your generosity, I am seeing my own.

There is nothing that we are drawn to in another that is not already a part of ourselves. So when you see qualities in others that you admire or love, you are seeing the aspects of yourself that are wanting and ready to come forth. When you see qualities in your partner that you hate, that piss you off, you are seeing the parts of yourself that you have buried away. If your mate's lack of integrity upsets or angers you, it is because you can't be with your own lack of integrity. You're either denying it, hiding it, or suppressing it.

Many of our disowned traits are acted out in our marriages; when our relationship comes to an end, we are left with a lengthy list of what is "wrong" with the other person. Our task is to name these qualities, to reclaim them as our own, and to honor them as an integral part of ourselves. We must be honest enough to feel and heal these wounded aspects of ourselves. Only then can we take responsibility for our part in the failure of our relationship.

The Universe, in its unconditional love, helps us to see ourselves for who and what we are, even if it's through the actions of an unpleasant mate. When we trust that both the "good" and the "bad" in us are God-given traits, we can begin to heal by reuniting with all of the qualities that we've stuffed away. Until then, we will see in others what we like and don't like in ourselves. Inevitably we attract partners and other people into our lives who mirror back these disowned parts of ourselves. If I hate my husband's greed, my task is to find the greedy part of myself. It's helpful to understand that my greed may show up differently than it does for my husband. I may want all the food on the buffet table, or I may want to take credit for other people's projects at work, while my husband's greed shows up as hoarding all the profits from the family business.

Sometimes people get stuck in this process because the quality they hate in their partners is one that they feel they've never displayed. For example, if your partner has deceived you by having an extramarital affair and you know that you have not been unfaithful, it may be difficult to find your own deceit. In this case, it is necessary to look and see if you have displayed the quality to yourself. In order to uncover this hidden aspect of yourself, you may need to ask, *When or how have I been deceitful to myself?*

Every quality that affects you in a negative way is one that you are displaying—either with others or with yourself. It would be impossible for us to find these aspects in ourselves if we didn't have other people to show them to us. So our mission is to search out and find all the parts of ourselves that we have hidden away out of shame.

UNDERSTANDING YOUR EMOTIONAL BUTTONS

As a child, your deepest need and desire was to be loved. So when your mother told you it was not okay to be angry after you punched your little sister, you may have taken the part of yourself that was mean and hidden it away. When your father said, "Idiots don't make it in life," you took the innate idiot in yourself and stuffed it behind your "know-it-all" facade. Every family has its own standards for what is acceptable and what is not; to fit in and be accepted in your own family you had to figure out which parts of yourself were unacceptable and hide them away.

Imagine that being sexy and outspoken were two traits that were not tolerated in your family. Today you would probably have a difficult time speaking out or embracing your sexuality. It could be that being a wimp and being too sensitive were the no-nos. So you grew up trying to be tough in order to fit in and be loved. As we grow up, we hide and suppress more and more of ourselves until we no longer know all of who we really are. The message ingrained in our psyches from our parents, family, friends, and religious leaders is that it's not okay to be all of who we are. And if you do show us all of you, you'll be deemed unlovable and unacceptable. Ashamed, you will take these so-called bad qualities and stuff them away deep into your unconscious.

To understand this concept more clearly, imagine that every quality on the planet is represented as a button on your chest. One button is labeled "loving"; another says "sensitive." There is a button for "arrogant," "manipulative," "joyful," "controlling," and "honest." The qualities within you that are healthy and healed have electrical cover plates over them. They are neutral, free from charge, and have no energy coming forth from them. For example, if you see someone being rude and rudeness is not an issue for you, you'll notice their rudeness, but no negative energy will rush through you. You'll be *informed* by their behavior, but not *affected* by it. But the qualities in you that are unhealed—that have been denied, hidden, or suppressed—have energy coming from them. If lying is an issue for you, hearing someone tell a lie will trigger an emotional reaction in you, sending a jolt of negative energy throughout your body.

The only way to heal this reaction and put a cover plate over this hot button is to understand that what you're affected by in your partner is really an unhealed part of yourself. The emotional energy surging through you serves as a guide, showing you where you are wounded and separated from yourself. These fragmented parts act out to get your attention and remind you that they have not yet been healed. Your job is to reclaim and integrate these parts of yourself and extract the wisdom they contain. Only then can they become part of your whole being. And only then will these unconscious hot buttons lose their power over you.

TAKING BACK OUR PROJECTIONS

Here's how it works. We draw people into our lives to see the parts of ourselves that we have denied. Instead of accepting our disassociated parts, we project these qualities onto our partners. Projection is a defense mechanism of the ego. When our partner does something that disgusts, annoys, or affects us in any other negative way, that behavior is actually a mirror of ourselves.

It's difficult to know when we are projecting. When I was married to Dan, I was infuriated by what I perceived as his unwillingness to work on our problems. I saw myself as completely willing to work on our relationship, but after many hours of introspection I came to realize that, as much as I professed willingness, I was only really interested in working on Dan. I believed that if he were fixed, my problems would go away. Though I couldn't see it at the time, I too was unwilling to work on myself. I projected my unwillingness onto Dan.

Once we take back our projections, own our hidden parts, and release our toxic emotions, something magical happens and our internal world shifts. And when we shift how we feel about ourselves, our partner's behavior toward us automatically shifts as well, reflecting the change.

Robin and Richard, on the brink of divorce, came to see me for some individual coaching. In the heat of their fights Richard always blamed Robin for putting him down and not finding him worthy of being her life partner. In our work together, when Robin came clean with her inner dialogue, she admitted that deep down inside she never felt that she had married the right man—a man who was good enough for her.

When Richard decided to disconnect and stop blaming Robin for his feelings, he began to look for the unworthy aspect of himself that Robin continually mirrored back to him. It didn't take long for him to see that since childhood he had felt unlovable and unworthy. He had worked hard to find a partner who would make him look good in an effort to cover up his own feelings of inadequacy. To the outside world Richard had succeeded, and everyone thought him a lucky man to have captured such a beautiful and charming bride. But left unhealed, his deep-seated feeling of unworthiness continued to haunt him throughout his entire nine-year marriage. Now, with that marriage in jeopardy, Richard was willing to search for deeper understanding and personal healing and had come to see just how Robin mirrored back the aspect of himself that he had tried so hard to hide.

In one session I asked Richard to close his eyes and remember a time when he had felt unworthy or unlovable. What appeared before his eyes was his parents' divorce. When Richard was six years old, his father left without a look back. Richard blamed himself for the un-happiness of his parents, including his father's rejection and his mother's depression. He decided that he was inadequate and unworthy of hav-ing the people in his life love and honor him. He became a victim of his own interpretations, and he could now see that this had become a painful theme in his life. When he finally decided to take ownership of these upsetting emotions, he was able to stop blaming Robin for mak-ing him feel unworthy and to embrace the feelings of unworthiness as his own. Once he did this, he no longer needed Robin to mirror back his negative self-image.

Taking back our projections and taking responsibility for them empowers us to come to a new place in the present. Richard stopped downplaying his capabilities and decided to make his own life great so that he could be proud of himself. He reclaimed his own sense of worth. Robin could feel his reclaimed power and no longer had to add to Richard's negative feelings.

Our mate can only plug into our wounds when they are left un-healed. No one can get us upset unless we have an unresolved issue from the past. If we didn't have toxic feelings stored up, we would not react to our mate's upsets, complaints, and grievances—we would merely listen. We get angry and reactive when we have unresolved issues that need and want resolution. It is the power of negative projection that destroys good relationships and our ability to love without judgment and condemnation.

Some of you are already aware of the hidden parts of yourself. Some of you have buried these aspects so deep that it is unfathomable that you could possibly possess these intolerable aspects. But whether you are aware of them or not, the process of finding and healing all of ourselves is sacred and holy. Such healing allows you to meet yourself and God in every person, in every action, and in every incident.

Part of the process of evolving and returning to our natural authen-tic state is reclaiming all aspects of ourselves, the good and the bad, the dark and the light. We are the victim and the victimizer, the heartless and the heartfelt, the caring and the uncaring. And at some point in our lives, when we are pushed to our limits, even if we've been successful at showing only our best side, our evil twin will surface. That's why some of us see traits in our partner that we have never experienced before.

BALANCING THE SCALES

Michelle had been married for twelve years. After eleven years of ignoring the extramarital activities of her husband, Steve, she woke up one day and decided that she'd had enough and wanted a divorce. Suddenly this very sweet, overly accommodating woman who had been passive for years turned into an intolerant, angry bitch who was unwilling to put up with any of her husband's behavior.

Steve went into total shock: he couldn't comprehend how Michelle could suddenly want to break up their family after years of not saying a word about her unhappiness. In Steve's mind, he didn't even mean to take advantage of her blindness. Meanwhile, all the anger and hostility that Michelle had suppressed for years surfaced. The aspects of herself that had been buried away since she was a young girl were taking over.

A part of Michelle wanted to get help and see whether she could work it out with Steve, but she was unable to control her temper with Steve or her children. I asked Michelle to imagine a seesaw, with one side up in the air and the other side down on the ground. She could see that it was out of balance. I told her that this was exactly what was happening inside of her. When she had been passive, ignoring Steve's behavior, she was out of balance; now she was in the other extreme, enraged and acting out aggressively.

Emotional wholeness is having your passive side and your aggressive side in equal balance. Both aspects are imperative to the whole. With access to all of herself, Michelle could balance her passive self at one end and her aggressive self at the other. It is only when we have access to both sides that we are able to make the highest evolutionary choice at any moment. If Michelle embraced both sides equally, it would be just as easy for her to speak her truth as it would be to let things go. Yet until she could access and appreciate each of these vital aspects of her personality, only one part of her personality would come out at a time, and only in the most extreme circumstances. Looking back, Michelle can see that aggressive or assertive behavior by a woman was unacceptable in her home. Turning the other cheek was the way her mother dealt with her straying father.

This story is more than common. The circumstances may be different, but at some point these disowned aspects will pop up, hitting us in the face. Think of your disowned aspects like a beach ball. Do you know how much energy it takes to keep a beach ball under water? You must spend all of your energy trying to keep it submerged. Then, the moment you take your energy away, it pops up, splashing water in your face. All the aspects of ourselves that we hide and deny are like beach balls buried beneath the surface of our consciousness. They usually wait for the most inopportune time to pop up and hit us in the face, exposing the parts of ourselves that we have worked so hard to hide.

When we take our attention off ourselves and point a finger at our partner, we are able to transfer our self-hatred. It is important that we expose our disowned parts and bring them into our conscious awareness. Our partners have come into our lives to teach us many things. Unfortunately, most people don't know how to learn the lessons, so they repeat the same kind of patterns in one relationship after another. To find freedom we must come to understand that we co-create every situation and that our experiences of others are reflections of the healed or unhealed aspects of ourselves. Only then can we move beyond the point of anger and depression and into the liberating world of personal responsibility. Taking back our projections gives us back our independence and the power to be our own healers.

HEALING ACTION STEPS

1. Make a list of all the negative qualities in your partner that you find irritating, painful, or offensive. Include those traits that anger, enrage, or disgust you.

2. Make a list of all the negative qualities in your parents or primary caregiver that you find similarly upsetting.

3. Close your eyes and ask yourself, *Where in my life am I displaying this quality?* It will probably look different in your life than it does in the life of other people. If you can't find any place in your life where you are displaying this trait, go back into your past and remember a time when you expressed it.

4. Next to each of the negative qualities you listed, identify your judgments about each one. For example, if you wrote that your husband is a liar, your judgments about that quality might look something like this:

Liars are bad.

My father was a liar.

People who lie are evil.

People who lie need help.

People who lie will hurt me.

Chapter Seven

MAKING PEACE
WITH OURSELVES

He who angers you, conquers you.

ELIZABETH KENNY

The Law of Responsibility governs the choices we make. There's no accident in who we are attracted to and why we married them. It's in the seeds of our karma. Every person we attract into our lives is there to move us to the next phase of our personal evolution. They behave in whatever manner is necessary to show us the places where we need healing and make us confront the issues that prevent us from fulfilling our potential. When we take full responsibility for our lives, we understand that the relationships we find ourselves in are not mere accidents but custom-designed opportunities to heal our emotional and spiritual wounds.

Karmic relationships, by definition, are relationships that are meant to be. A relationship is karmic whether it's traumatic, abusive, happy, satisfying, or purely sexual. Our soul's vibratory frequency creates a field of resonance that surrounds us and attracts those people who vibrate at the same frequency. If you have issues with being abandoned, you vibrate at a particular frequency, and you attract people in the same frequency who will abandon you. Until you heal this wound, you will continue to attract people who bring it to your awareness.

There are no accidents. Understanding the energetic resonance of our souls is essential to being able to cut the karmic cords that keep us tied to our partners in negative ways. If we don't understand the energetic resonance of our souls, we won't understand why we attract certain people into our lives and why these people act in particular ways. To complete the process of taking responsibility we must acknowledge that, at some level, for some reason, we attracted our partners into our lives.

There were over one thousand people attending the conference where I met Dan. After only a few minutes of talking, we made a connection that would ultimately change our lives and lead us to our wedding day. Although neither of us knew it at the time, Dan held the key that would open up many doors in my inner world. I can now see that Dan was the catalyst for me to go deeper into my healing process. He opened the door to motherhood for me and at the same time showed me all the places inside where I was unhealthy and wounded. My ex-husband embodied many qualities that I was unaware of within myself. He showed me many parts of myself I had never before seen. Our karma together moved me to San Diego, gathered my family together in California, and gave me the experiences I needed to write this book. And these are only a few of the ways in which my life has changed as a result of partnering with Dan. When major events such as these occur in connection with someone, we know our relationship with them is karmic.

THE PROCESS OF BECOMING WHOLE

The person to whom we ultimately commit our lives is there to mirror back to us our true selves. They are carrying, so to speak, some aspect of our humanity that we have disowned. Our partner unconsciously reflects the disconnected parts of ourselves that we are blinded to.

It's imperative to understand that you are not designed to find these aspects alone. You have probably spent most of your life unconsciously trying to hide these aspects of yourself, but when summoned, they will come out. The fragmented parts of yourself long to be integrated and healed, and finding and healing them must be done with great compassion. The most important part of the valuable process of healing and loving all of yourself is to be willing to look beyond what you can see and past what you know about yourself.

The process is threefold. The first step is to identify what you like and don't like about your partner. In order to do this, you must distinguish between qualities and behaviors. Let me give you an example. Let's say that you just found out your husband is seeing another woman, and you hate that about him. If I tell you that this is a part of you, you immediately say, "But I am not like that. I would never cheat on him. In fact, I've never cheated on anyone."

But you must go a step further by asking this question of yourself: "What *kind* of person would cheat on their spouse?" Everyone will come up with a different set of words. You might come up with the word "weak," "mean," "insecure," "self-centered," "selfish," "angry," "unfaithful," or "dishonest." List one or all of the words that you come up with yourself to describe the quality you are seeing. If you are leaving your wife because she is a workaholic and you feel that you are well balanced, you would again ask, "What kind of person would be a workaholic?" Your response might be "perfectionist," "obsessive," "overachieving," "fearful," "cold," "driven," "selfish," "egotistical," or "insecure."

It is vital that you keep asking yourself what kind of person would engage in the behavior you dislike so that you'll be able to see beneath the behavior. Underneath all behaviors are the qualities that drive them, and that's what we're looking for.

Jo Ellen is thirty-eight and a divorced mother of two. After five years of watching her husband, Dave, work late nights and watch sports on the weekends, Jo Ellen felt so lonely and hopeless that she decided to end their nine-year relationship.

Jo Ellen prided herself on the way she ran her household. She was up early every day with her children and spent the evenings helping them with their homework. She worked full-time as a high school teacher, yet she rarely missed her daily workouts. Everything in her life had a time and a place, and she reveled in her daily routine. The day when Jo Ellen could no longer hide from the glaring differences between herself and her husband was the moment when she deemed their marriage irreconcilable.

In Jo Ellen's opinion, Dave never helped out with the children, worked all night, and exercised only if he was competing in a softball game. When Jo Ellen made her list of the qualities she disliked in Dave, she initially saw no similarities between herself and her husband. But as she became more willing to see how they were alike, her list gradually began to shift. Her biggest complaint about Dave was that he paid so little attention to the family. When I asked her what kind of person would pay little attention to his family, the words Jo Ellen came up with were "uncaring" and "selfish." So I asked Jo Ellen if she loved herself when she was selfish and uncaring. Immediately her defenses went up, and she insisted that she was never uncaring or selfish. Her reaction was a dead giveaway that we had just hit upon two disowned and unhealed parts of herself.

Step two is distinguishing a disowned trait from a trait that we simply observe in another person. In the book *Meeting the Shadow,* Ken Wilber says, "If we are just receiving information about someone's behavior it is probably not a projection." If you observe someone being careless and you merely receive that information without judging it, you are probably not projecting. However, if you are affected by the person's behavior—if you are upset or angry or feel you must point your finger in blame—you are probably projecting an unhealed aspect of yourself. The minute we say, "I'm not like that," we must acknowledge that the behavior we're judging reflects a part of ourselves from which we have separated. Remember, we have every quality within us, so figuring out what we're projecting points us toward those parts of ourselves that are in need of healing.

When you've made your list of qualities that you know you're not or that you don't want to be, the next step is to own these parts. By "owning" I mean finding and accepting these aspects in yourself. You don't have to like them or love them at this point; you just need to be honest with yourself and admit where and when you have displayed these qualities.

To find these often buried parts of ourselves we have to go into the silence of our deepest self. Our psyches are brilliant and, when asked, will expose their truth. Imagine having hidden a coin in your house when you were two years old. Would you remember that you hid the coin? Even if someone confirmed that you had hidden the coin, would you remember after all these years where it is? This is what it's like for most of us. These qualities are buried deep within our subconscious, trying to stay out of sight.

To see whether Jo Ellen was ready to own "selfish" and "uncaring" I had her close her eyes. I asked her to take a few breaths while I asked her this question: "When or where in your life have you been uncaring or selfish?" Within moments, with tears in her eyes, Jo Ellen recounted the story of her mother's death. Jo Ellen and her mother had had a turbulent relationship for years; they never seemed to agree on anything, and they rarely got along. Jo Ellen believed that her mother was too selfish to have had children. When her mother was diagnosed with terminal cancer, Jo Ellen did not reach out to support her mother but instead turned toward her own family and gave very little to her mother in the last months of her life. Jo Ellen had blocked this from her memory, and the realization and the images that she saw in her own mind stunned her. This uncaring part of herself had been buried in her consciousness for a very long time but was so vivid for her now that it was as if no time had passed. She began to see that Dave's behavior mirrored her own selfishness and that, like Dave, she had her own excuses for acting the way she did. Jo Ellen was distraught for weeks because she hated these parts of Dave and hated that she possessed the same horrible qualities. Her constant question was, "How can this be?"

Often the pain that accompanies the discovery of one of these disowned parts of ourselves is excruciating. It stings like salt on an open wound. This is because we are drowning in our righteous indignation, having made others wrong for behaviors that we're sure we are incapable of. Now, shockingly, we've come face to face with our evil twin, something that most of us don't want to see. I know this is not an easy process, but the benefits are so great and the healing so necessary that we must breathe deeply and know that as soon as we locate the gift of this unwanted part, the pain will disappear. Once we have owned our painful truth, we no longer have to be controlled by the outer behavior of those around us.

After we own our disowned traits, we are ready to move to step three. This final step leads us to embrace the gift of these unwanted qualities. For Jo Ellen, embracing the gift seemed like an impossible task. She told me that to see anything good in these qualities she would need a miracle, a complete act of God. For her entire life she had always blamed someone else for being selfish and uncaring. First it was her mother and then her husband. I explained that one definition of a miracle is a shift in perception. If Jo Ellen was willing to see the gifts that "selfish and uncaring" had to offer her, she could have a miracle. All she had to do was to be willing to see *both* sides of these qualities. I recounted one of my favorite stories, told by Guru Mayi, the leader of the Siddha Yoga Foundation.

The ruler of a prosperous kingdom sends for one of his messengers. When he arrives, the king tells him to go out and find the worst thing in the entire world. The messenger returns days later with nothing in his hands. Puzzled, the king demands, "What have you discovered? I don't see anything." The messenger says, "Right here, Your Majesty," and sticks out his tongue.

Bewildered, the king asks the messenger to explain, and the messenger responds, "My tongue is the worst thing in the world. My tongue can say many horrible things. My tongue speaks evil and tells lies. I can overindulge with my tongue, which leaves me feeling tired and sick. My tongue is the worst thing in the world."

Pleased, the king then commands the messenger to go out and find him the best thing in the entire world. Days later the messenger shows up again with nothing in his hands. The king shouts, "Where is it? I don't see anything." The messenger replies, "Right here, Your Majesty," and sticks out his tongue. The messenger tells the king: "My tongue is the best thing in the entire world. My tongue is a messenger of love. Only with my tongue can I express the overwhelming beauty of poetry. My tongue teaches me refinement in tastes and guides me to choose food that will nourish my body. My tongue is the best thing in the world because it allows me to chant the name of God."

The act of transformation is seeing something one way and in a moment being able to see it in another way. One view generally empowers us, and the other view disempowers us, leaving us feeling weak and vulnerable. We get to choose. To find the gift is to allow ourselves to see from all perspectives, to see all sides of the qualities we possess.

Imagine that you can only experience the harmful aspects of your tongue. You would miss a million of life's pleasures. The same is true for all your qualities. You might ask, what is the gift in being uncaring? Being uncaring can help us survive: it allows us to draw healthy boundaries and attend to our own lives. If you were always caring for everyone else, it is likely that you would not have time to take care of a family of your own or a career other than one of complete service to others. You would probably be driven to care for all the millions of sick, starving, and less fortunate.

The process of reclaiming ourselves is not easy. Most of us are very attached to the way we see things because our view and opinions are what distinguish us from others. One very interesting exercise is to interview five people who know you well. Ask each person to tell you the three things they like the most about you and the three things they like the least. It never fails that a quality described by two or three people as positive is reported in a negative light by another person. For example, one person might say that he likes your straightforwardness, but another person says that she doesn't like it that you always speak your mind, adding that "some things are better left unsaid." Reality is an interpretation. Looking through different eyes generates different perspectives—and therefore different realities.

In a state of enlightenment we can see all views at the same time. When we shift the way we see something, we let go of our limiting beliefs and the painful reality that goes along with it. Shifting our views allows us to go from happy to sad, from upset to peaceful, in an instant. This is the process of embracing the gift of any trait. We all know that we can look at a glass as half empty or half full, and that both views are correct. The same is true for each part of us. It is ultimately our choice whether we stay focused on a trait as empty and devoid of value or as full of possibility and potential. We can choose to hold on to our belief that some of our so-called personal characteristics are bad, or we can choose to look for the greater purpose of each and every aspect of our personality. It is the ego that dwells on the negative aspects of our humanity. It is our higher self, the holy and sacred part of us, that chooses to look beyond what we know to find the gift of our shadow.

When Jo Ellen was finally ready to find the gift, she had already taken the most important step in the process. She became willing to let go of her beliefs and harsh judgments and see another view. In fact, she was more than willing; she was desperate and hungry for a new perspective, so her entire being was open to finding one. She closed her eyes while I asked her to find the gift of her selfishness. I guided her to allow whatever words came to her to be the exact right information she needed. I encouraged her to not think about this process, but rather to surrender her will and ask her highest self to be her guide.

After several minutes Jo Ellen opened her eyes and told me what she heard and the images that came to her mind. She had suddenly realized that her selfish self gave her the greatest gift of all—the drive and desire to be selfless. Because she didn't want to seem self-centered, Jo Ellen did volunteer work, headed up the PTA at her daughter's school, and was always available for friends in need. In an instant Jo Ellen was able to see that "selfish" had driven her to bring out many positive qualities because of her intense desire to be viewed as selfless by others.

Now that she could acknowledge this part of herself, it just needed to be thanked and viewed in a new light. Jo Ellen needed to bring her selfless side—her kind, forgiving, light side—to her dark judgments of "selfish." Then she could shine a loving and accepting light on this part of herself. Once she could accept and embrace this quality, she no longer had to judge it when she saw it expressed in Dave. Regardless of what Dave contributed or failed to contribute to their family, Jo Ellen was now informed by his behavior rather than affected by it. Through Jo Ellen's commitment to her own inner work, she gave herself the greatest gift of all: freedom to choose her response to Dave.

Whether we want to see it or believe it, the parts of ourselves that we hate the most are the ones that are running the show. In a strange, backward way, everything we don't want to be drives us to become the opposite. This is how our shadow self camouflages itself. All you have to do is close your eyes for a moment and think about a part of yourself that you love or like a lot. After you have found that part, ask yourself, *What is the opposite of this quality that I love?* You will immediately see a quality that you don't love and that you don't want to be. It's this very quality that you don't want to be that drives you to be who you are today. It's the act of covering up the unwanted aspects that makes up your positive personality.

Martha loved her humor. When she asked herself what the opposite of "funny" was, the word that arose from within her was "serious." Martha had always had a distaste for serious people, and, of course, she had a very serious father whom she never wanted to emulate. Harold loved his adventurousness. When he looked, he saw the opposite as fearfulness. He had never imagined that he had a fearful bone in his body, but his wife and mother were both professional worriers. Because Harold couldn't bear to be fearful and weak like his mother, he had to create a persona so strong on the other side that no one would ever question his courage. Jeffrey liked his cool nature. He was always hip on everything, owning the best gadgets, cars, and clothes. He was the star of the L.A. social scene, and what he despised most were geeks. The geek in Jeffrey, which he admitted to displaying until age twelve, was unpopular and lonely, so Jeffrey created himself to be so cool he'd never be left out again.

Often the gifts are this obvious. The gifts of your shadow self are often seen in the qualities you love most in yourself. Your personality wasn't created out of wanting to be something; rather, it was born from *not* wanting to be a few particular things.

Amazingly enough, most of us find a partner who demonstrates the very qualities we've tried so desperately to stay away from. Now we are at a crossroads where we are given the opportunity to heal and embrace all of our shadow qualities. If we choose to turn our backs on this task, we have to live with the fear that they could show up another time, in another place. And they will.

DISCOVERING THE GIFTS

Going within and exploring our inner world opens us up to finding all our hidden treasures. As Carl Jung said, "The gold is in the dark." Each time we bring a disowned aspect of ourselves into the light of our consciousness, we are given back a gift much greater than any one of us could imagine. It's like taking off rose-colored glasses after wearing them for ten years. Suddenly everything looks different. The world and its inhabitants are no longer familiar, yet there is something very exciting about all the new colors and textures.

The same thing happens when you step out of the trance of projection. Everything looks and feels different. The behaviors of your past are gone, and other people's actions seem different to you in this new light. Suddenly all the negative cords that have bound you to your partner in disempowering ways are released. The little things that he or she says to you no longer bother you, and you no longer need to keep your guard up. Finding these gifts is like digging through a treasure chest—you always find unexpected gems.

You must be prepared to love all that you have feared. Even though exploring this new terrain can feel like standing on shaky ground, it is only a matter of time before you feel the comfort and stability of the earth beneath your feet. And this earth will feel very different from anything you've ever experienced, because its foundations are made up of love, compassion, and emotional wholeness.

When we open the door to our inner world, we discover a menagerie of personalities—many selves with many faces. For each characteristic or personality trait there is a subpersonality that emerges in order to give us access to each unique part of our psyche. Roberto Assagioli, founder of psychosynthesis, says, "We are dominated by everything from which our self becomes identified. We can dominate and control everything from which we disidentify ourselves." Examining our subpersonalities is a tool to support us in reclaiming the lost or hidden parts of ourselves. It is also a way to heal the aspects of ourselves that may be acting out in rage or have been saddened with depression.

Assagioli devised a method for disidentifying with these parts of ourselves so that we can hear their vital messages. When allowed into our consciousness, the voices of our unembraced qualities can be our guide and our partner in bringing us back into balance. This process enables us to find the gifts in our darkness.

MEETING OUR SUBPERSONALITIES

The first step in subpersonality work is identifying and naming each of your hidden aspects. Assagioli suggests that when you disengage you develop a relationship with these aspects so that you can heal and integrate them into the whole of yourself. Naming each part of yourself allows you to create distance and to view each part in a different light. For example, if you don't like the judgmental part of yourself, giving it a name like "Judgmental Judy" helps you disidentify with it in order to open up a dialogue. Then, when you find yourself judging your partner, instead of feeling bad that here you are again being judgmental, you can close your eyes and talk to Judgmental Judy. You can say, *Hey, here's Judgmental Judy again. Maybe she needs a little attention or a loving chat to mellow her out.*

Giving the disidentified parts names softens our harsh judgments of them. It allows us to see them as separate from ourselves so that we can take them out of the personal realm and experience them in a nonpersonal way. This immediately supports us in stepping out of the harshness of thoughts like *I am judgmental*. Once we name our subpersonalities, we can begin to work with them.

The next step is to close your eyes and give your disidentified parts an image, a face. This is very easy to do, because your psyche is designed to give you information with pictures. If you don't see a face for a particular quality, you can always conjure up an image of someone you know or someone you've seen on television who would fit into the role of this quality. With the name and face intact, you can then begin to have a dialogue with this part of yourself.

The first experience I ever had with subpersonalities came in a Transpersonal Psychology class at JFK University. My teacher, Suzanne West, led us in a guided visualization in which we imagined boarding a big yellow bus filled with people. When we got on the bus, we were instructed to take a seat and go for a ride. Then she suggested that someone was tapping us on the shoulder and that it was one of our subpersonalities. She then asked us to stand up, walk around our bus, and meet all the other subpersonalities standing in the aisles, lying on the floor, and shouting out the windows. Even the bus driver was a subpersonality.

As Suzanne spoke, I allowed different facets of myself to emerge from deep within my awareness. I saw a tall, skinny teenager and a loudly dressed, middle-aged drunk. I saw sad, happy, and scary-looking girls and a few crying children. On my bus were literally fifty different personalities, all trying to capture my attention. At some point Suzanne told us that our bus would soon pull over and that one of our subpersonalities would come to take us off the bus for a talk. The woman who walked up to me weighed approximately two hundred pounds and had thinning gray hair. She wore a sweater around her neck held in place with an old rusty clothespin. She was dressed in a beige muumuu with large orange polka dots. She reeked of cigarettes and hair spray. My first thought was, *Oh my God, I'm not going anywhere with* her. But when I voiced my opinion, she looked directly into my eyes and advised me that she was the only one there, and if I wanted to do this exercise, I should follow her. So I did.

Sitting next to her, I asked her name. She quickly replied, *Big Bertha Big Mouth.* Appalled, I tried to stay focused and listen to the teacher's instructions. The next question we were to ask of our subpersonality was: *What is your gift to me?* Without a pause, Big Bertha advised me that she was trying to move me to the next level of my spiritual path. Since this was something I really wanted, I started to pay more attention.

The next question for our new friend was, *What do you need to be whole or to integrate into my psyche?* Again Big Bertha was quick to respond: what she needed was for me to stop judging people by the way they looked. Feeling defensive, I quickly told her that I had been on a spiritual path for over five years, and I no longer judged people by the way they looked; that was a behavior of my past. And then came the shocking response that changed the direction of my life forever. Big Bertha Big Mouth, my subpersonality whom I had met only moments before, said, *I am just a figment of your imagination, and because of the way I looked, you didn't even want to go for a walk with me.*

Wow. She was right. I sat there stunned. I would have never been able to own up to this behavior, because I had convinced myself that I was no longer doing it. But here I was, busted inside my own mind. To this day I'm not sure which part was harder to digest—that I could have so much wisdom coming from inside of me or that I could be in so much denial that I didn't even know I was still judging others by the way they looked.

The bus represents the totality of our being, and each of the faces on my bus represented a different aspect of myself. Each one was waiting for the opportunity to be heard and to become an integrated, healthy part of the whole. This experience was eye-opening. It left me with a deep inner knowing that, indeed, "the answers are within." I had heard it so many times, read it in so many books, but I was still going outside of myself to get the answer whenever I had a problem. Now, without a doubt, I knew that if I was willing to get quiet and listen, I could gain access to the wisdom I needed to heal.

This exercise sent me off on a tangent. I quickly made a list of all the parts of myself that were giving me trouble, acting out, or being reflected back to me by others, and I set out to get to know each of them. Each one came bearing a different gift and had different information to help me heal. They gave me two recurring messages: *I want you to stop hating me,* and, *I just want to be appreciated for the gifts that I have given you.* Whatever their face, their size, or their shape, whether they spoke with gentle words or bopped me over the head, every subpersonality within me wanted respect and forgiveness. As I met more and more aspects of myself, my heart softened and I was able to feel great empathy for these lost and lonely souls.

The more familiar I became with these different parts of myself, the more things in my life began shifting. The continuous negative chatter that had filled my head got quieter. Instead of projecting my harsh judgments onto other people, I began to feel more compassion for them. Putting faces and names on these qualities changed my relationship with them. I no longer had to beat myself up when I was displaying a behavior I didn't like. If I woke up feeling angry, I would immediately call forth "Angry Alice" and give her a face that would allow me to feel sweet toward her. Then I'd ask her what she needed from me in order to feel better. Every time I asked for help, one of my subpersonalities would tell me exactly what I needed to do to shift my feelings and my behaviors.

SEPARATING THE PERSON FROM THE PERSONA

An important component of creating a Spiritual Divorce is finding ways to tolerate our partners' quirks and learn to make peace with his or her irritating behaviors. Subpersonality work helps us to separate the person from the behavior. If we can't separate the personality traits of our partners from their being, we will continually be judging them and assaulting their character. By identifying and naming these aspects, we begin to relate to our partner in a new way: we separate the person from the persona. Automatically the grip that has held us hostage loosens up, releasing the emotional charge that has been causing us distress. When we give faces and names to the parts of our partner that have been driving us crazy, we stop taking his or her personality personally.

Jane and David were going through a turbulent time in their marriage and needed to find a way to communicate with each other without the harshness of their judgments. Attacking each other's character by saying things like, "I can't stand living with you because you are lazy," was getting them nowhere. I asked each of them to make a list of their partner's bothersome qualities and then to name them as subpersonalities. Here is what they wrote:

DAVID'S SUBPERSONALITIES

Lazy Louie

Irritating Irving

Steven the Stoner

Oblivious Ollie

Peter the Pretender

Walter the Weakling

Asshole Andy

Spineless Caesar

Frank the Flake

Dick the Dreamer

Disgusting Douglas

Marvin the Mama's Boy

Gutless Gus

Bankrupt Bart

JANE'S SUBPERSONALITIES

Wigged-Out Wanda

Scarlet the Scatterbrain

Helen the Hypochondriac

Paula the People-Hater

Controlling Connie

Inconsistent Inga

Insecure Selma

Pitiful Paula

Blanch the Blamer

Addicted Alice

Selfish Sylvia

There is an old story that says when you arrive in heaven, they take your heart in one hand and a feather in another. If your heart is lighter than a feather, you know you have reached a state of enlightenment. Subpersonalities, with their names that amuse you and faces that make you smile, can lighten you up. If Nasty Nick shows up to pick up your children, instead of getting yourself all charged up you might just say to yourself, "Oh, look who's here, it's my old friend Nasty Nick."

Take the time to have some fun and know that we all have our own cast of characters and personality problems. Going within and dialoguing with subpersonalities changes your life forever. In the book *Conversations with God,* God reminds us, "If we do not go within, we go without." We are each filled with an infinite amount of profound wisdom, and in times of distress it is imperative that we reconnect with our divine nature and allow the spirit of the Universe to be our guide.

I am often asked, "Why am I the one who has to do all the work? Why do I have to deal with these same issues over and over again?" The answer is simple. You have to do the work because ultimately you are the one who receives all the benefits. It does take time and effort to make peace with yourself. It's not an overnight process. As far as I can tell, it is a lifelong pursuit. When you commit to emotional wholeness, you are committing to being there for yourself every day, not just once a week when you go to the therapist or the chiropractor or when you take time for meditation. You give yourself the gift of knowing that you can count on yourself and take care of yourself. You wouldn't leave a child outside in the rain for a day, so why would you leave the wounded child within you alone without care and attention for a day, week, month, or year?

Close your eyes now and bring forth an image of yourself when you were four years old. Imagine that you are unhappy and scared. Would you pick that child up and hold her in your arms or would you scream at her and tell her to get over it? Would you be comfortable treating the child the way you treat yourself now? Would you say the things that you are constantly repeating to yourself to this precious child? Is this what you deserve?

Whether you want to believe it or not, you are that child. You carry all of your selves at all ages with you every day. Learning to love yourself is the greatest task you will ever be given. Giving yourself love is the greatest gift you will ever receive. But it takes time, care, persistence, and patience. It takes the compassion of an innocent heart and the dedication of an Olympic athlete.

HEALING ACTION STEPS

1. Take the list of your partner's negative qualities from exercise 1 in chapter 6 and make them into subpersonalities by giving them

names. Using the following visualization, see whether you can discover the gift that each quality has to offer you. If you have a hard time finding the value of a particular trait, keep asking. Often the gift of a particular quality expresses itself as the opposite value.

2. Set aside some uninterrupted time to do this visualization. Before getting started, you may want to take a walk or enjoy a long bath to relax yourself. Consider playing some soft music or lighting a scented candle to create a peaceful mood. Close your eyes and begin by allowing your awareness to rest on your breathing. Take a few long, slow, deep breaths, retaining the breath for five or more seconds and then slowly exhaling. Do this four or five times until your mind becomes quiet.

Create in your mind's eye the image of a large yellow bus. Imagine yourself boarding the bus and taking a seat somewhere in the middle. Feel the excitement of embarking on a long-awaited trip into yourself. As the bus pulls away from the bus stop, look out the window and notice that it is a clear and beautiful day.

As you ride along, enjoying the scenery, you begin to notice the other passengers on the bus. You see people of all sizes and ages—tall people, short people, children, teenagers, and old people. You see that the bus is filled with people from all walks of life. There are circus people, homeless people, business people, even animals. Some are waving to get your attention while others may be hiding in a corner. As the bus pulls to a stop, you get up from your seat and begin walking down the aisle, taking in all the characters on your bus. Now the bus driver tells you to let one of these characters—one of your subpersonalities— take your hand and escort you off the bus and into the park.

Imagine yourself sitting down next to this person. Notice the quality that he or she seems to embody. If it's someone fearful, you could name this person Fearful Franny or Fearful Fred. If the person doesn't give you his or her name, you may come up with one based on the person's appearance or most prominent characteristics. Notice how the person is dressed and how he or she looks. What does the person smell like? Notice his or her mood and body language. Now, taking another deep breath, look directly at the person and ask, "What is your gift to me?" Keep asking until you get a response. After you have received the gift, ask the person, "What do you need to be whole?" or, "What do you need to be a healthy, integrated part of me?"

After you have heard the response, ask the person, "Is there anything else you need to say to me?" Then take a moment to acknowledge the subpersonality, this fragmented part of yourself, for being willing to share with you. Imagine yourself walking the person back to the bus. When you are ready, open your eyes and write down the messages you received from your subpersonality. Continue writing for at least ten minutes about your experience during this exercise.

THE LAW OF

CHOICE

Chapter Eight

WALKING IN ANOTHER'S SHOES

Life is not the way it's supposed to be, it's the way it is.
The way you cope with it is what makes the difference.

VIRGINIA SATIR

The way we feel about our life is the result of the interpretations we have made. The Law of Choice opens us up to the realization that there are many ways we can interpret our life's events, none of which are true. All of our pain and suffering is created by how we view our present circumstances. Although we do not always have the power to choose our life's events, we do have the power to choose our interpretations of them. There are two kinds of interpretations—those that empower us and those that disempower us. The Law of Choice guides us to view our lives from a new perspective and to create new interpretations that empower us to act rather than react. Then we become the designer of our new reality.

It's imperative to realize that everything—every action, every behavior, and every person—looks different through different sets of eyes. I began to understand this principle while attending a seminar many years ago. We were instructed to stand up and look around the room. We were given a few minutes to notice and observe all the different objects in the room. We were then instructed to sit down in our chairs and view the room again from a seated position. Next, we observed the room while standing on a chair, and, finally, we ended up lying on the floor and looking around us. From every position we observed new things. There was an amazing difference between the way the room looked when I lay on the floor and how it looked when I stood on the chair. Every time I changed position my focus went to different things, and my experience changed.

In order to heal we have to look at our relationship and ourselves from different perspectives. We need to explore new viewpoints and arrive at new judgments. This is what it means to have free choice, or free will. As individuals, we are free to view life from many possible angles. Many of us don't realize this. We get caught up in the reality we see at the moment and believe it to be the only truth. We become victims of our own perceptions, which limit and color what we see. Many of us have learned to interpret our lives in disempowering and devaluing ways.

One of the first changes in my perception came in the middle of my divorce when I shifted my focus from Dan to myself. Instead of trying to analyze Dan's actions, I began to question my own. Why would I respond in certain ways, and why would I draw a man into my life who would do and say these particular things in this exact way?

It is my deepest belief that the external world is a mirror of my internal world, so when I don't like what's going on outside, I always go to work to change what's going on inside. In my marriage I constantly took the attention off of myself and put it on Dan. But now, in order to heal and have a supportive, healthy relationship with Dan, I would need to change my perceptions and turn the finger I had pointed at him back toward myself. I began to look at everything that was going on around me. How was I being treated? How was I spoken to? I noticed the constant internal dialogue that always told me I was right and Dan was wrong. I observed my defensive nature and my own resistance to hearing what my partner had to say. I noticed how shut down I was to hearing the advice of others, how unwilling I was to have my marriage work in spite of what I was telling myself. Every time I didn't like what I saw or heard on the outside, I would close my eyes and go inside to discover the lessons I needed to learn.

The first and most important lesson I needed to learn was to stop looking from the narrow perspective of my ego. My ego told me I couldn't make it alone with a child. It told me to be careful and to get as much as I could out of Dan because for sure I wouldn't have enough. The eyes I was viewing my world through were small, scared, and concerned only with myself. When I decided to shift my focus, I began to think not only about Beau and myself but also about Dan and how he would survive. Even though at this point we disagreed on almost everything, I spent time in daily prayer sending love and healing energy to Dan. I felt that even though I couldn't see his perspective, it would be an important lesson for me to try to understand his pain and his choices.

One day, after a morning of frustration and rage, I decided to try seeing life through Dan's eyes. I took some slow, deep breaths, closed my eyes, and tried to enter the mind of my soon-to-be-ex husband. This was a difficult task, as you might imagine, since Dan was the last person I wanted to be at that moment. I began thinking about how we met and about the feelings that were present when we decided to get married and have a family together. As I opened myself up to viewing our relationship from a different point of view, I could feel the anxiety fill my body. It startled me to look at our relationship through a different set of eyes. Part of me begged to go back to the safety of my own small, righteous reality, but I pressed on, trying to imagine how Dan might feel.

I started from the beginning, when I moved to San Diego. Looking back, I tried to remember things Dan had said to me. I tried to imagine how it would be to work my entire life to save money and become comfortable in a particular lifestyle. Then I meet a woman who I imagine will fulfill my fantasy of a happy family life. Then I propose. With great hope and much joy, she and I begin making plans for our future together. Then the day arrives when she moves into the house I love.

After she finally gets settled and we begin to merge into a happy couple, she proclaims that my dream home and the town I live in make her miserable and unhappy. She decides that we have to sell my home and move to another town more to her liking. At the same time we find out that she is pregnant with the child we both desire. We celebrate and continue creating our dream. But weeks later she becomes very sick, and suddenly everything about me is wrong. The dream dies before it ever really begins.

It didn't take long before I realized how difficult it must have been for Dan to live with me. Until that moment I had never even considered his view. My view had been all that mattered.

To cut the karmic cords we must be able to see life through the eyes of our mate. Until we can do this, we continue living in a self-centered reality. Unless we are willing to understand the other person's perspective, we continue to make ourselves right and our partner wrong. The cords continue to bind us to each other until we have learned the lessons that have brought us together. We can evolve and grow only when we are willing to give up our narcissistic view that things are only as we see them and try to understand the experience of life through the eyes of the other.

Susie was trapped in the painful, narrow view of her divorce. She was thirty-five, fun-loving, and the mother of four. She had spent most of the previous seven years raising a family and supporting her husband, Roger, in building a successful law practice. One day Roger came home from work and told her there was something he needed to discuss. After putting the children to bed, Susie went into the family room to talk with Roger. She sensed that something was wrong but figured that he had had a hard day at work or lost a big case. When Roger began to speak, what came out of his mouth were words Susie never expected to hear: "I'm sorry. I never meant for this to happen, and I don't know how to tell you this, but I've fallen in love with another woman."

Susie sat there, stunned and unable to move or speak. She listened while the love of her life, her soul mate, and the father of her children rambled on about his affair and how he was going to move out of the house so that he could move in with the other woman. With his head hanging down, he quietly muttered that the other woman was pregnant with their child. Roger assured Susie that this was never his intention. He told her that she would have nothing to worry about—of course he would take care of her and the kids.

A year later Susie was still trying to recover from what she considered the worst beating of her life. After moving out and filing for divorce, Roger had fought for as much of their mutual property as he could get his hands on. His promise to take care of her and their children had vanished, and now it was up to the court to set a compulsory amount that he would have to pay to Susie for child support and alimony.

After a year of tears and enormous bouts of anger, Susie knew that she had to let go of the pain. Not only was it affecting her, but the children were suffering from emotional outbursts and discipline problems at school. She had read many books, listened to tapes, gone to church, and prayed to her higher power, but nothing seemed to help. When she came to see me, she was praying for a miracle.

The miracle Susie needed was to heal and move on. There was nothing she could do to change the past. Her husband wasn't coming back. And for now, the security that she longed for was gone. When Susie was ready, I had her write a letter from her husband to herself. For a few minutes she needed to step out of being herself and into being Roger. I asked Susie how Roger had felt being married to her. What would Roger say? Susie wrote the following letter:

Dear Susie,

I loved you from the very first time I saw you. No matter what's happened, I never intended for our marriage to end this way. I got caught up in making money, and you seemed to be totally occupied and content being a mother. There was never time for our relationship. You seemed to have lost interest in sex. The kids always came first, as they should. When Jessica came along, I lost all control. I had met a woman who was interested in my career and me. I'm sorry, I just didn't have the strength to stop. Please forgive me, Roger.

For Susie, writing the letter revealed how lacking in sexual enjoyment she had been since the birth of their first child; how little time she really had for Roger's needs because she always put her children's needs first; and, to her surprise, how little interest she really had in Roger before the split happened. Seeing their life together through Roger's eyes gave Susie some clarity and understanding. She now had the choice to use this new information either to beat herself up or to transform her life.

EXPERIENCING OTHERNESS

Until this point Susie had chosen to believe that she was a victim. She felt ugly, worthless, and helpless. She felt jealous that Roger had chosen a woman who had a successful career and was in great physical condition. Susie was drowning in her own pain, and it would take an experience of "otherness" to rescue her. Otherness invites us into the lives of others. It's an experience you can have only if you dare to step out of the limited "me" perspective and step into the experience of another. The ultimate goal of a spiritual life is to take you beyond your ego, beyond the world of your own small self, and into the presence and comfort of your divine self.

In the midst of an ugly custody battle, James could see only the hateful, angry, vindictive side of Sandy. During the four years since their separation, James had felt like the victim of his ex-wife's vindictive nature. She had even gone so far as to accuse him of acting inappropriately with their twelve-year-old daughter. This shocking accusation from a woman he once loved sent James into the darkest feeling he had ever experienced.

Just the mention of Sandy's name, a call from the lawyers, or an innocent comment from his children sent James into a frenzy of toxic emotions. He had collected piles of evidence to substantiate that all his negative beliefs about Sandy were true. The problem was that it didn't matter whether all the nasty things were true or not because, either way, they were ruining his life. His resentments toward his ex-wife were affecting his intimate relationships and interfering with his loving connection with their children.

The goal of my work with James was to find a place where he could at least feel some compassion for Sandy and have an experience of otherness. He knew that his negative feelings toward her only fueled the fire that raged between them. I asked James to write a letter from his ex-wife to himself, and after much resistance, this is what emerged.

Dear James,

I felt really secure being married to you because I knew that I didn't have to worry and that was a tremendous relief to me. You supported me in the tasks of living. I miss that in my life now. I am fighting for the kids because I feel in my heart of hearts that your influence will take them away from me. And I don't know if I could live without them. They are all I have to live for. Please understand this and forgive me.

Sincerely, Sandy

Amazingly, we can always see another person's perspective if we are only willing to look. After doing this exercise, James suddenly had a sense of Sandy's pain. Even though he still hadn't resolved many of his angry feelings toward her, for the first time in four years James actually had the experience of otherness. Writing the letter opened his heart to her, and he was able to look at their situation with new eyes—eyes that included both his world and that of his ex-wife.

When we broaden our perspective, choose new interpretations for our experiences, and see through the eyes of another, we gain supports in the difficult process of taking total responsibility for our lives. New interpretations assist us in finding the hidden meaning behind traumatic or unpleasant events. We can reinterpret negative events so that they empower us and support us in moving forward. When we walk through life carrying the load of our unwanted past, filled with painful memories and unexpressed emotions, we are weighed down. We feel a perpetual cloud of heaviness hovering over us as we wait for the next problem to arise. Our opinions get stronger, and a sentiment of seriousness permeates our world.

MAKING CONSCIOUS DECISIONS

Shifting your perspective allows you to choose from a new place where you are empowered rather than disempowered. The decisions you make now will affect the rest of your life. Unless you consciously choose your interpretation, you may shut down in some way for fear of getting hurt again. It's imperative that you acknowledge that you do have a choice in how you view your divorce, your partner, and yourself. You have the choice to see your ex as an enemy or as an ally. This is your opportunity to examine your interpretations and invent new perceptions to reconcile your experiences. Doing so will enable you to expand rather than contract your capacity for love.

Have you ever gone to dinner with a friend who is down on his luck and who sits and moans about being dealt a bad lot in life? Maybe he complains to you about how badly he's been burned by a lover or boss? How do you feel with that person? Are you inspired to go out and emulate him, or do you feel sorry for him? Do you feel lighthearted and cheerful in his presence, or heavy and sad? Everyone at some time in his or her life will receive a bad blow. It is not the incidents themselves that cause us pain, but rather what we decide about each event.

Emotional pain arises out of how you choose to interpret the events of your life. If you have been sitting around excited by the idea that your spouse might cheat on you because it would finally motivate you to get a divorce, when he does you'll be happy. But if you thought you were going to spend the rest of your life in marital bliss, or at least married, the news that your husband is having an affair probably causes you terrible emotional pain.

The severity of your pain is always consistent with the number of similar unhealed events lingering like open wounds in your emotional body. If you have been left many times before and have never reinterpreted and healed those events, they will remain, adding fuel to the fire of your present heartache. Your pain level is different depending on whether this is the first or the fifth time this has ever happened to you. Dr. Patrick Dorman, creator of the "Mind Gardening" process, says, "When you have a lot of emotional baggage, it clouds your ability to interpret events in empowering ways."

How you look at your past and at the decisions you make surrounding your present circumstances changes the way you deal with life now and in the future. Each person's pain is different. You cannot compare divorces or divorce stories. You cannot compare levels of pain. Everyone has a different tolerance level for different experiences because each of us sees through different eyes. Two people can go through a difficult experience, and one will use it as an opportunity to strengthen his or her inner resources, while the other uses it as an excuse to drink or take drugs. We can't always choose what happens to us, but because we are blessed with free will, we can always choose how we are going to interpret each incident and how we are going to use it to go forward in our lives.

INVENTING NEW INTERPRETATIONS

The events in our lives have no inherent meaning. We are the narrators and the ones who give them meaning. We decide what each event means and how it will affect our lives. Each interpretation we choose to apply either adds to the quality of our life or takes away from it. Each negative event either opens our eyes to an opportunity to change the course of our life for the better or sends us into a bottomless pit of pain, suffering, and self-abuse. Self-sabotage is birthed out of our woundedness and indicates that we are carrying unresolved emotional issues that need to be healed. Our self-destructive behaviors are there to remind us that something in our lives is calling for our attention. Creating positive interpretations challenges our view of the world and shifts the way we see ourselves and others.

The next step I took with James was to look at the interpretations that were undermining his relationship with Sandy. We began with his core belief: "Nothing I can do will ever make Sandy happy." James could see that as long as he held on to this view, it would never be possible for Sandy to be happy or satisfied. It cut off all possibility for her to ever show up differently. I explained that our interpretations act as a filter, weeding out anything that isn't compatible with our belief.

For example, if you interpret your partner as someone who is closed-minded and compulsive, you bring that filter, which consists of certain attitudes, ideas, and beliefs about him, to every conversation you have with him. In all your interactions you listen to him through the filter that says he is compulsive and closed-minded, and your beliefs cause you to experience him that way. It is almost impossible for him to show up differently because your filter automatically shuts out any information that is contrary to your belief. Anything he tries to do or say that runs contrary to your beliefs simply isn't registered in your mind. This refusal to register contrary information allows your ego to validate your righteous opinions and gives you the satisfaction of being right.

Our experiences set up our beliefs—and our beliefs set up our reality. Since we can't go back and change our experiences, if we want to change our reality, we must change our beliefs. This is the step that allows us to change the dynamics of our relationships and behaviors and to alter our future reality.

Our minds are powerful creators; we fill them with either thoughts and beliefs that build us up or thoughts and beliefs that break us down. If James had continued to hold on to his negative beliefs about his ex-wife, eventually they would have not only destroyed his relationship with Sandy but damaged his relationship with his children.

The only way I have found to loosen the grip of the embedded negative interpretations that drain our life force is to exaggerate the underlying interpretation that filters our experience. James needed to reinterpret his belief that nothing he could do would ever make Sandy happy. I asked James to make up three new negative interpretations about Sandy that were even worse than the one he already had. Then I asked him to invent three positive interpretations of her. At the end of the exercise we could decide which interpretations left him feeling angry, resentful, and disappointed and which ones helped him feel strong. He would then be free to create the possibility of a healthy, stable co-parenting relationship between two adults with a common bond.

JAMES'S NEGATIVE INTERPRETATIONS OF SANDY

1. Sandy wants to regress and to have me become her father. She wants my entire life to be about taking care of her. She wants to make my life a living hell.

2. Sandy wants me to give up my life and be suffocated by her needs.

3. Out of spite, Sandy will withhold her vulnerability to show me what an inadequate loser I am.

JAMES'S POSITIVE INTERPRETATIONS OF SANDY

1. The gift of me not making Sandy happy is that now she has to make herself happy. That gives me full responsibility for my own happiness.

2. Sandy's determination to never let me make her happy drives and motivates me to find peace of mind at a higher level.

3. Not being able to make Sandy happy strengthens my resolve to succeed in the world and find constant bliss in unexpected places.

James looked at all of his new interpretations and acknowledged that any or all of them could be true. From this new vantage point, James decided that he no longer wanted to carry the burden of his old, disempowering interpretation, so he chose instead the interpretation that "not being able to make Sandy happy strengthens my resolve to succeed in the world and find constant bliss in unexpected places."

James turned next to reconsidering the interpretation that "Sandy's mission in life is to seek my utter and complete annihilation."

JAMES'S NEGATIVE INTERPRETATIONS OF SANDY

1. Sandy's job is to torture me by sabotaging everything that matters to me—my parenting, my love life, and my libido.

2. Sandy's life is committed to turning me into a woman-hating, angry, unsatisfied man.

3. Sandy's job in life is to humiliate me and make me wrong.

JAMES'S POSITIVE INTERPRETATIONS OF SANDY

1. Sandy's constant battering makes me a humble, detached person in an enlightened way, forcing me to surrender to my higher self.

2. Thanks to Sandy, I am a better lover because I know its opposite, and my knowledge of what it's like to be without love strengthens my loving nature.

3. Sandy gives up being a kind and loving person to inspire me to be the opposite. Viewing her self-imposed misery teaches me to create more and more love in my life.

James again agreed that all or none of these interpretations could be true. He chose the interpretation that, "thanks to Sandy, I am a better lover because I know its opposite, and my knowledge of what it's like to be without love strengthens my loving nature." This interpretation made him laugh and feel good about Sandy.

To change our perceptions we must search our past and create powerful new interpretations that allow us to take full responsibility for the events of our lives and find the blessing that each moment brings. It takes time and effort, yet the benefits can transform our relationships and our lives. Many people want to forget about their past, but Friedrich Nietzsche tells us that to wish away our past is to wish ourselves out of existence. Instead of wishing our painful past away, we need to reinterpret our beliefs about each event so that we can be grateful for the experiences we've had.

There is an old saying, "Life is a school to the wise man and an enemy to the fool." If we look at life as a school, then all we ever need to ask is: *What do I need to learn from this? Why did I need to have this experience? How can I use this experience to enrich my life?*

John McShane, a renowned divorce attorney, recently shared with me his quest to encourage his clients to have a Spiritual Divorce. He believes that everyone can choose this path if they wish to learn from their experience and their partner. John encourages his clients to work hard during this difficult time and to heal the deepest parts of themselves.

John shared his own philosophies about life's problems with me. Most of us resist our pain, but John takes the contrary view: "I like to know I'm getting a good deal, so I always try to maximize my pain. I'll be damned if I'm going to go through this pain without getting the value from this. I want to harvest all the benefits." He sees that whining, bitching, moaning, or indulging in rage robs us of the opportunity to get the most out of our pain. It's our responsibility to get the most out of all the events that knock on our door. We can succumb to the ease and familiarity of victimhood, or we can challenge ourselves on the path to greatness.

Last year I worked with a couple who were at risk for getting a divorce. Because each was carrying a lot of resentments toward the other, they were unable to live in the present and to foresee a future together.

Calling it quits seemed easier than continuing in the same patterns that had plagued their marriage for many years.

We began by uncovering the core beliefs that drove their behaviors toward each other. Allen was sick of Deana's constant complaint that he didn't make enough money and that she should have married a rich man. In his interpretation of Deana's complaining, Allen had formed the belief that "I'll never make enough money to satisfy Deana's expensive taste."

Allen's interpretation disempowered him and left him feeling that the only alternative was to get divorced so that Deana could finally find her rich husband. His feelings of unworthiness triggered his constant anger toward Deana. I wanted him to see that Deana was simply expressing her frustrations and desires with money and that he himself, not Deana, was choosing to make her words mean "Allen will never make enough money to satisfy Deana."

Even if Deana herself agreed with this interpretation, Allen had the choice to use her dissatisfaction to empower or disempower himself. I wanted him to understand the power of choosing interpretations and to have the experience of seeing that many choices were available to him. I coached Allen in creating some new negative interpretations of Deana's behavior that would be worse than the one he already had. He came up with these.

ALLEN'S NEGATIVE INTERPRETATIONS OF DEANA

1. Deana is out to torture me and ruin my life. She wants to suck every penny out of me so that I'll die broke.

2. It's my job to sacrifice all my needs and desires in order to fulfill Deana's self-centered, egotistical ways.

3. Deana is lazy and selfish, and it's my job to do everything for her while she does nothing.

Then I asked Allen to make up some positive interpretations for Deana's behavior. I encouraged him to be creative and to try to come up with interpretations that made him smile even if they seemed ridiculous. He created these:

ALLEN'S POSITIVE INTERPRETATIONS OF DEANA

1. Deana loves me more than any other person could love me in the entire universe. She keeps her internal conversations about having a rich husband alive so that I can work through my issues and become the best person I could ever be.

2. Deana is in total awe of my capabilities and talents, and she knows that I am destined to produce amazing things in the world. Her internal conversation supports me in discovering my real truth.

3. Deana wants a husband who is rich in love, passion, and appreciation for the wonderful things that exist in the world.

Now that Allen had written down six new interpretations, I asked him to identify the ones that empowered him and those that didn't. It was easy to see that any of these interpretations could be true, and that it was ultimately up to him to choose the lens through which he wanted to view Deana.

I guided him to choose one interpretation that made him feel good. He chose "Deana loves me more than any other person could love me in the entire universe. She keeps her internal conversations about having a rich husband alive so that I can work through my issues and become the best person I could ever be." Allen could see that this might really be the truth, but because of his unhealed wounds around money, any time Deana expressed her fears, desires, or concerns about their financial situation Allen immediately made it mean something bad.

We moved on to the next issue that kept Allen from having an intimate, loving relationship with his wife. He had decided that Deana's many mood swings were due to the fact that she was manic-depressive. By constantly suggesting that she seek professional help, Allen left

Deana feeling sick and pathetic. Allen created these new interpretations to explain Deana's emotional states.

ALLEN'S NEGATIVE INTERPRETATIONS OF DEANA

1. Deana uses her emotions to drain my energy and to suck the life out of every cell of my body because she hates me.

2. Deana is truly crazy and in denial. She wants to ruin my life.

3. Deana is so emotionally irrational that my life is unmanageable. As long as I am around her, I will be off center, and it's all her fault.

ALLEN'S POSITIVE INTERPRETATIONS OF DEANA

1. Deana is a savant and beyond normal interpretation.

2. Deana is very passionate about living and expresses it in what seems to be manic-depressive behavior.

3. Deana is a truly spiritual person, and she energetically interprets her experiences in an intense and extreme emotional realm. I learn so much from her.

Again Allen saw the value of examining and creating new interpretations. He saw that he could use any or all of these interpretations and that it was ultimately his choice to be either disempowered or empowered by the interpretations he chose. Allen chose to interpret Deana's behavior as "Deana is a savant and is beyond normal interpretation."

When examining your interpretations, you must ask yourself, *Does this interpretation empower me or disempower me? Does this interpretation make me feel weak or strong?* If you are left feeling weak by your perceptions, you need to examine your internal dialogues and replace them with positive, powerful conversation that leaves you filled with hope. To do this exercise effectively you must write down each and every interpretation. Doing it in your head won't work. The act of writing down your interpretations allows you to see them with your own eyes and begins to shake loose the negative emotions that are tied to your circumstances.

Consciously choosing our interpretations supports us in having an extraordinary life. If we hold on to our negative views about our partners, we continually see them through judgmental eyes. Our limiting beliefs not only keep us firmly linked together but continually create more disappointment, pain, and resentment. You may be saying, "But my ex-wife really is a selfish, lazy bitch." What I am suggesting is that none of the interpretations we choose are true—not the ones we have now and not the ones we are going to invent—because through different sets of eyes, every person, every place, and every event looks different. You may consider your ex-wife's behaviors lazy or bitchy, but I guarantee you that not everyone experiences her in this way. What's important to see is that when you hold on to negative views, they suck your vital energy and rob others of the opportunity to change in your presence.

Deana's turn came, and she wanted to heal the negative interpretations that were keeping her from experiencing her love for Allen. The first belief that fueled Deana's resentment was that "Allen doesn't love me enough to give me the lifestyle I desire."

DEANA'S NEGATIVE INTERPRETATIONS OF ALLEN

1. Allen hates me so much that he wants to make sure that every day I have on this planet I experience deprivation and feelings of unworthiness.

2. I am such an evil, disgusting sleazy bitch that God sent Allen to torture me and make sure I repent for all of my sins and experience degradation and suffering every day of my life.

3. Allen thinks I am a selfish, spoiled, undeserving, crazy, hysterical woman.

DEANA'S POSITIVE INTERPRETATIONS OF ALLEN

1. Allen wants to support me in reaching my highest potential and to give me the experience and fulfillment of attaining success on my own.

2. Allen believes in my talent and capabilities and wants me to express myself fully. Not fulfilling my desire to be taken care of is his way of supporting me.

3. Allen wants me to be his partner in creating a rich life together instead of just giving it all to me.

Deana was amazed at how much better she felt just from doing this exercise. By inventing and writing out new positive and negative interpretations, it is easy to see the silliness of getting stuck in a position that makes you feel bad. Deana chose: "Allen wants to support me in reaching my highest potential and to give me the experience and fulfillment of attaining success on my own."

In the light of all her new interpretations, Deana could see that this was indeed exactly what Allen would do to support her in fulfilling her potential. She was used to having a father figure to take care of her, yet her dependence always left her feeling bad about herself. She wanted more money so that she could fit in with all their wealthy friends. But Deana was different from the people she hung around with and always had a deep desire to help others and make a difference in the world. On a very deep level she knew that Allen would do anything to support her in reaching this goal.

Understanding the power of our interpretations is an essential part of the healing process. We don't necessarily choose new interpretations to be kind to our partners; we choose them to be kind to ourselves. Even though seeing another through new eyes is one of the nicest gifts you could ever give that person, we choose to see through new eyes so that we ourselves can feel strong. Looking through new lenses opens up a whole new range of possibilities for ourselves, our children, and the people we are separating from. This is the process of taking responsibility for what we see and how we feel. No one else can do it for us. We must do it for ourselves.

I choose to believe that my ex-husband will do whatever I need him to do. It doesn't always look that way in the outer world, but it sure makes me easier to deal with. And it's an interpretation that leaves me feeling like I have a partner and friend rather than an adversary.

HEALING ACTION STEPS

1. Write a letter to yourself from your partner. It's important to do this at a time when you feel somewhat calm. Go for a walk or watch a funny movie before entering into this task. When you feel ready, take out a piece of paper and a pen and set them nearby. Close your eyes and take five slow, deep breaths. Allow yourself to imagine your partner sitting in front of you. Give yourself permission to become your partner. Breathe in your partner's persona, and when you're ready, open your eyes and begin writing: "Dear (your name). . . . " From that moment on, don't think—just try to be your partner and see what he or she says about what it was like being married to you.

2. Write down all the negative interpretations you have about your partner. Here are some examples:

- My husband is an unfit father.

- My wife is an emotional basket case.

- My husband would sell his own mother to make a dollar.

Now make up three new interpretations that are even worse than the ones you already have.

3. For each of your old interpretations, create three new positive interpretations. If you need help, review this section in the chapter. Now choose the interpretation of your partner's behavior that leaves you feeling strong and empowered.

4. Write your new interpretations of your partner's behaviors on index cards or sticky notes and display them in places where you will see them often. Do this to remind yourself that "reality" is an act of interpretation and that you can choose at any time to interpret your life's events in empowering rather than disempowering ways.

Chapter Nine

THE WEDDING GIFTS

Perhaps everything terrible is in its deepest being
something that needs our love.

RAINER MARIA RILKE

Once we choose new interpretations, we can begin the process of embracing the gifts of our marriage. Whenever we've been betrayed or disappointed, it's natural to hold on to our pain as a defense mechanism. The voice of anger and hurt always tells us to watch out and be careful. Our pain hardens our hearts and clouds our vision, blinding us to the gifts we have received from our marriage and our divorce. The Law of Choice gives us the freedom to go beyond our past and beyond our negative feelings. It provides us with the tools to look with new eyes at the experiences our marriage provided. The Law of Choice states that we have the power to choose to view our breakup either through the eyes of suffering or with a heart of gratitude.

At this point you may not feel like you are quite ready to be grateful, but your alternatives are bleak. As long as you deny the lessons and gifts that your partner has been trying to give you, you continue to be tied to the very thing you want to break free from. "Setting others free means setting yourself free," says the great spiritual leader Emmett Fox. "When you hold resentment against anyone, you are bound to that person by a cosmic link, a real, though metal, chain. You are tied by a cosmic tie to the thing that you hate. The one person perhaps in the whole world whom you most dislike is the very one to whom you are attaching yourself by a hook that is stronger than steel." Even though you think your anger, hurt, disappointment, and resentment are well deserved, unless you are prepared to carry this person on your back everywhere you go for the rest of your life, you may want to consider forgiveness as the *only* solution to becoming a whole, complete, free person.

When I first began to understand how my resentments bound me to the people I most disliked, I found it almost comical. My intention had been to use my anger to protect myself from being hurt again by those persons who had hurt me before. My bruised ego wanted to create distance between me and my enemies, yet instead of taking something away from them, I was giving them my most valuable asset. By resenting them, I was giving them my energy as well as complete and total power over my emotional well-being.

Simply the mention of my enemy's name or a reference to a similar story would set me off. It took no more than seconds to trigger all the bad feelings lying dormant within me. In an instant the person I resented had the power to join me wherever I was. I could be at a party, on a date, or at the supermarket, and if the wrong words were spoken, that person would pop right up in the forefront of my mind, accompanied by all the toxic memories of my past.

These toxic feelings were always with me whether I was conscious of them or not. Someone once told me that you must forgive the people you truly dislike or hate, for only then are they completely out of your consciousness. If you love them, hold on to your resentment and you will be able to bring them with you wherever you go.

We belong to anything we are linked to in a negative way. The frequency currents that hold our negative thoughts in place are so strong that they continually draw forth similar negative experiences. The negative implications of our hate are astounding. Our old resentments drive all our relationships. They tell us how close we can get to others and how thick the walls need to be to maintain emotional safety. They inform our daily behaviors, telling us how many risks we can take. And they build an invisible fence of protection around our hearts.

This kind of safety, however, is an illusion. We are never truly safe from hurt and pain, which is simply a part of life, of living and growing. All living things must grow or they die. The mature leaf crumbles to the ground, creating a space for new growth. My ex-husband said it beautifully the other day: "There is no change without loss." To fully protect ourselves from loss would literally mean that we close the door to all of life's possibilities.

The closest we can come to feeling safe is by trusting and believing that we can and will take care of ourselves through any storm. We are safe when our hearts are filled with love and compassion. We are invulnerable to attack when we are resting in the magnificence and enormity of who we are. If we are kind, nourishing, and loving inside, we attract others who mirror back that love.

Choosing forgiveness is a necessity for good emotional and mental health, for like attracts like. If you choose to come from a place of gratitude and forgiveness, you begin to vibrate at a higher frequency and naturally draw others in who reflect that back to you. If your heart is filled with love and compassion, you continually elicit that love and compassion from others. Similarly, if your mind is full of resentment and judgment, you attract others who are resentful and judgmental or who magnify your emotional pain.

Only you can choose to receive the gifts of your marriage. Otherwise, they remain unopened and unused. Looking at your life through a lens of gratitude allows you to receive the gifts and learn the lessons from your time with your mate. The lens of gratitude is always there. It may need to be dusted off, but if you want to, you can choose to look through it at any time. Finding and embracing your wedding gifts allows you to cut all the karmic cords that link you to your partner in a negative way. Then you can choose to go on with your life.

I work with many people who have been divorced for a long time, some for as long as twenty years, and who, even after marrying someone else, are still married in a karmic way to their first partner. Justin was married to Danielle for twelve years. When he found himself ready to leave his marriage, he reached out for some help. The first thing we did together was a short visualization exercise to determine what unhealed emotional wounds were connected to his desire to leave his marriage. To Justin's surprise, the person who showed up in his awareness was not his current wife but his first wife, Helen. He had been divorced from Helen for over seventeen years, yet when he looked inside himself, what appeared were all of the unresolved issues he had from his life with her.

They had separated on bad terms; Justin had lied about a lot of money matters. He had stolen a valuable camera from Helen and sold it to get money for drugs. Justin was still carrying his crime with him, even though he had not thought about it for over fourteen years. I explained to Justin that it would be difficult to see clearly the issues he had with his present wife until he cut the karmic cord with his first wife.

When he closed his eyes and asked his higher self what he needed to do to complete this marriage, he realized that he needed to replace the camera he had stolen and write a letter thanking Helen for leaving him. Helen's decision to end their marriage had been the catalyst Justin needed to finally get off drugs, and the divorce had taught him many valuable life lessons. It was the beginning of a new chapter in his life. Justin had straightened up and made the decision to emulate Helen and her family by becoming financially responsible. For many years he had done just that, earning a good living, paying his bills, and saving for the future.

With appreciation in his heart, Justin located and purchased the exact camera he had stolen, packed it with his letter, and sent it off to Helen asking for her forgiveness. A month went by, and Justin was basking in the joy of cleaning up his past. As he took care of his old relationship, something magical began to happen with his current wife. For the first time he was able to be present and to see the many ways in which he had created the same kind of relationship with Danielle that he had with Helen, except that this time the tables were turned. Now Justin was playing the role of Helen, the responsible, sensible partner, while Danielle was clearly acting out as he had in his past, by being financially irresponsible. Now that Justin had cut the karmic cord that tied him to his ex-wife, he was able to complete this part of his life and take responsibility for the condition of his current relationship.

The experience of karma is having our attention in the present impinged upon by experiences from our past. That is why it is imperative that we complete and heal all of our relationships. Until we do, we keep the past alive by continually bringing it into the present.

Until we embrace the gifts we received from our marriage, the karmic link to that relationship remains intact. Burdened with the pain of our past, we continue to drag our unhealed emotional issues with us wherever we go. Our past drains the vitality out of our future relationships. What's more, our past is a constant reminder of our fears and all our pain. Holding on to our past is a sure recipe for re-creating similar situations until we learn the lessons that our partners have been trying to teach us. If we don't acknowledge the gifts we were meant to receive, they remain unopened and unavailable to us.

Often I hear, "I've learned the lesson, but I'm not glad it happened." I would suggest that if you feel this way, you have not really received the gifts and embraced the lessons of your marriage. When we have truly learned the lessons taught to us by our former mate, we appreciate and value the experience no matter how difficult it has been. We integrate the experience and use it to make ourselves better people. Once we have digested our experiences, we turn them into a resource that contributes to who we are and how we feel about ourselves.

I guarantee that if you feel really good about who you are, you will appreciate everyone who has added to the recipe that made you. Honoring your experiences instead of dwelling on the pain fosters gratitude and rewards you with the joyous state of emotional freedom.

LEARNING THE LESSONS

Katherine's road to healing was long and painful. She had been married to Eric for fourteen years. Katherine was madly in love with Eric, even though he was emotionally abusive. In her experience, Eric was as crazy as Charles Manson one minute and as compassionate as Gandhi the next. It was the Gandhi aspect of Eric that kept persuading Katherine to stick around.

It was a difficult marriage in which Katherine earned most of the money and did most of the work of raising their three children. One day, after a week of Eric's erratic and abusive behavior, Katherine decided that living with him was no longer safe for her and the children, and she finally made the decision to leave. Even though Katherine still loved Eric, she could no longer justify being around his behavior. Scared to death of what he might do if he found them, Katherine chose to go into hiding.

Katherine realized that her idea of love was built on many misconceptions from her past. Eric's abusive behavior was similar to that of her emotionally abusive father. Since she had learned about loving men from her father, she was comfortable with someone like Eric, who treated her the way her father had. Katherine instinctively knew that the only way to get away from Eric was to leave town and hide from him. She feared for her life and the lives of her children.

The day came. Katherine woke up, got dressed, and walked out the door with their children, never to return. Abandoning her business left her in a financially compromised position. For a month Katherine lived on the lam, hiding in friends' homes and sleeping in small hotels in obscure parts of the state. Finally, out of desperation, she made the call to her family for help. To Katherine's amazement, her entire family rallied around to support her in making a new life. Then she received the surprise of a lifetime: her father flew a great distance to come get her and the kids. He met them at the airport in Chicago, paid for their tickets, and boarded a plane with them to Florida.

You would think that the awful experience of being married to Eric would have been enough, but it took Katherine another troubled marriage to realize that maybe all the chaos in her life had something to do with her. As soon as that internal lightbulb went on, she began to understand her participation in her life's drama. It took her many years of soul-searching to realize that the only way to break free from her past would be to take total responsibility for everything she had gotten herself into.

With gentleness and understanding of the wounded part of herself, Katherine took responsibility for permitting herself to be abused and for allowing these men into her life. She struggled past all her internal conversations that screamed, "But he did it to me, he is the sick one." She suffered through the difficult process of embracing the angry, cruel, confused parts of herself that she had seen and despised in Eric. She worked fearlessly to heal the wounds that were responsible for attracting abusive men into her life. Katherine was finally ready to learn the lessons that life was trying so hard to teach her.

Once she was ready to accept the lessons of her many destructive relationships, Katherine realized in a meditation that she had never considered healing herself from the inside out. She had always been the victim of life—first the victim of her father, then of a string of other difficult men. Her lesson was to learn to love and nurture herself, and to realize that she didn't need a man to be whole.

Most important, she discovered that she was not a victim. In many of her relationships Katherine had seen the writing on the wall but chose to ignore what she saw. Instead of looking for men who might give her lasting love, her lack of self-esteem always directed her to go for the quick fix, the moment of passion. Now, through her pain and loss, Katherine learned that she could stand up for herself and by herself.

When the time came to let go of all the baggage she had lugged around year after year, Katherine could see the gifts clearly. Her list of the gifts she had received from her partners looked like this:

1. I discovered how often and how harshly I abused myself with my own internal dialogues (*You are such a jerk . . . you're disgusting . . . you're so stupid*).

2. I received the profound realization that the abusive men in my life were mirrors of my own self-abuse.

3. By studying my ex-husband's behavior, I learned to identify my own core issues.

4. I learned that I am one of the strongest people on the planet and that there isn't anything I can't handle.

5. I now know that no matter how horrible the circumstances, I am never alone. I can call on God and get immediate relief.

6. I learned what a joy it is to raise my children without fighting, without having to take a vote, without arguing.

7. I received the gift of being able to raise my children with unconditional love, safety, and security.

8. I learned that being with the wrong person is much worse than being alone.

9. I received the gift of being able to come home at the end of the day and to know that I am safe.

10. I now know that I can help other people and that I have something special to give them.

11. I live every day with the joyful knowledge that I have turned my own life around.

If the gold is in the dark, we should look to the worst crimes perpetrated against us to find the real gifts of our relationships. When we take the time to claim our gold, we learn the most important lessons of our lives. The gifts are revealed through our acknowledgment of what we have received from our marriage, including things we've learned from our mate.

During my marriage I learned and experienced at least a hundred things that have contributed to my life. When I breathe them in and honor my life by honoring my experiences, I bask in the joy of emotional freedom. My list of the gifts of my marriage looks like this:

1. I have the child I always wanted.

2. I moved to beautiful La Jolla, California.

3. I get to be a parent to Beau.

4. My sister moved to La Jolla to be close to us.

5. I began working with Deepak Chopra.

6. I developed the Shadow Process.

7. My ex-husband paid off my school loans.

8. I was able to experience having a family of my own.

9. My parents moved to La Jolla to be near Arielle, Beau, and me.

10. I received enough money to stay home and write my first book.

11. I had the privilege of being the daughter-in-law of Bernice and Marty.

12. I've learned how to look at life through the eyes of another.

13. I learned that you don't have to go to Harvard to be brilliant.

14. I've learned how to share and include others in my life even if I disagree with them.

15. I've become more thoughtful in my words.

16. I received the inspiration for my second book.

17. I've learned to not verbalize every thought I might be having.

18. I've had the profound experience of seeing how others change as I change.

19. I learned that I could make it on my own with a child.

20. I'm learning how to be a good mother.

21. I've learned that co-parenting can be a joy.

22. I've learned that in conflict I need to keep the attention on myself.

23. I had the wedding I always dreamed of.

24. I've learned to ask for what I need.

How can I resent a man who has given me so many gifts? The gift of my son alone is reason enough to honor Dan for the rest of my life. Listing the gifts allowed me to see all that I had gained through my entire experience. At a time when I could see only pain and disappointment, looking for the good, the gifts, and the lessons opened me up to a place of authentic appreciation for my partner. It gave me a choice of realities in which to live. I could choose to remain in the painful reality of what didn't work, or I could choose to celebrate in the joyful world of gratitude.

DISCOVERING THE VALUE OF YOUR RELATIONSHIPS

Five years after the traumatic ending to their seven-year marriage, I sat with Karla and Antonio. It was a magical experience for me to sit with two people who were honoring their lives by honoring their experience together. I was curious as to why they kept their connection alive and why they were spending time and energy to sustain and heal their relationship. With no children, it seemed like a waste of time and a difficult task to pursue a broken relationship. So I asked them: "What has inspired you to continue repairing the damage done to each other in your marriage?" Antonio looked me in the eye and said, "The years I spent with Karla were important years. I did a lot of growing up, and I did it with her. To deny all I gained would be to throw away these valuable years of my life."

Both Karla and Antonio innately understood that whether they stayed in communication with each other or not, because of their time together they would always be intimately connected. My friend and teacher Dr. David Simon gave me the scientific reason for this phenomenon:

In quantum physics, when two subatomic particles collide, some energy and information is exchanged. And from that point on, whenever anything changes in one of the particles, it instantaneously has an effect on the other particle. Similarly, whenever we encounter someone or have any kind of relationship, we exchange energy and information with each other, and from that point on we are never the same person. Another way of saying this is that we are forever changed as the result of the encounter.

Our connection remains even though the form has changed.

To deepen their healing process I suggested to Karla and Antonio that they list the gifts they received from having been married to each other. For them it was the icing on the cake.

KARLA'S WEDDING GIFTS

1. With Antonio, I was encouraged to express myself, through writing and acting.

2. I came to a deeper appreciation of my femininity.

3. I developed a willingness to communicate my thoughts and feelings.

4. I developed a profound ability to "receive."

5. I developed an appreciation for Japanese culture and a love for sushi.

6. I was able to experience the "normal" family I always wanted—and to be the first daughter.

7. I had the opportunity to play out all my domestic fantasies— home-cooked meals, decorating, and entertaining.

8. Being with Antonio guided me toward the strongest connection to Judaism I've ever had by celebrating and observing Jewish holidays for the first time.

9. I received the support and encouragement to explore my entrepreneurial side.

10. I received validation that my desires are important.

ANTONIO'S WEDDING GIFTS

1. I had the chance to be with a woman as she discovered what she wanted and went for it.

2. I learned about making mistakes together, blaming each other, and over time taking responsibility.

3. We were able to support each other to grow, no matter how painful.

4. I had the gift of having a partner to cherish and love, and to be loved by.

5. I learned that my wife could be my best friend.

6. I learned how to keep a kitchen and cook for myself like I was royalty.

7. I got to vigorously study sensuality with my partner.

8. I cultivated a passion for the arts.

9. I learned how to file.

10. I had a great connection to a vibrant family—having sisters for the first time and nieces and nephews I love.

Choice gives us freedom. It gives us the miraculous ability to live the life we desire rather than one that has just landed on top of us. Living a life in which we can choose how we ultimately feel about every person, event, and situation is miraculous. When we make empowering choices, we live in the wonderment of being a human being. Choice enables us to experience the ease of independence and the grace of loving who we are. As long as we are victims of other people's behavior, we have no choice. We continue to live under the umbrella of our internal dialogues, the ones that make statements like these:

"If things were only different."

"If only he or she hadn't done this to me."

"If only the lawyers had given me better advice."

"If I had only had a different judge, everything would be okay."

"If only I had done this when I was younger."

Victimization prevents us from experiencing the gifts. If we don't learn the lessons we are presented with, we will repeat them. Allow me to repeat this: *if we don't learn the lessons we are presented with, we will repeat them.* In a moment of brilliance, Rollo May said, "Insanity is doing the same thing over and over again and expecting different results." Until we learn from our past, we will continue to ride the crazy-making cycle of repetition.

LIVING A LIFE OF GRATITUDE

As I was growing up, my heart never knew gratitude. I felt entitled to what I had and always wanted more. My discontent showed up in every area of my life. I had the wrong body, the wrong parents, the wrong siblings, I went to the wrong school and lived in the wrong part of the country. My boyfriend always had the wrong shoes, the wrong smell, or the wrong job. I felt that God, and the Universe, owed me more. No matter what gifts I received, they were always less than adequate. I believed that I was owed a better hand.

I can honestly say that most of my problems stemmed from my inability to appreciate what I had. My discontent fed the noisy internal dialogue that lived in my head. It never occurred to me that I could change my life by changing my attitude, that my unhappiness stemmed from my discontent, and that my discontent stemmed from my belief that I was entitled to a better everything. Having the wrong attitude drove me to search and find the dark side of life.

A lot of our conclusions about life keep us stuck in a state of entitlement. When we are viewing life through the lens of entitlement, we cannot receive our gifts. If we see only what has been taken away or what we don't have, we are engulfed in the smallness of our ego. Our ego feels that it deserves to have everything it wants—now. As a close friend of our ego, entitlement wreaks havoc on our emotional stability by filling our mind with righteous indignation. Entitlement hides the lens of gratitude and shuts down our appreciation for the everyday miracles of life.

Gratitude is the gift of an open heart. It is a divine state of being that comes from the great wisdom and understanding that everything is as it should be. Gratitude comes when you look at all that you have instead of dwelling on what you don't have. Gratitude is a self-generated love tool you can give yourself every day. When you choose to live a spiritual life, you come to understand that everything you receive is a gift. If you are blind to the gifts that have been bestowed on you, you are missing the opportunity to know God.

One day someone suggested to me that until I developed "an attitude of gratitude," I would probably end up just being another victim of an unfulfilled life. This statement struck deep at my core because I feared living a life without meaning, a life that made no difference. Then the revelation came that caused me to shift the lens I was looking through. I found out that gratitude is a choice, something that can be acquired through practice. The more I practiced, the easier it became. Then, instead of having to work constantly at viewing my world through gracious eyes, over time it became a more natural reality.

CHOOSING THE HIGH ROAD

Life is often difficult; it's not the bed of roses most of us were expecting. Each incident, each lesson, each roadblock is constructed to bring us to higher levels of awareness—to bring us closer to our spiritual selves. We are brought up in the illusion that our lives will turn out the way we want. And we believe that our fantasy reality will come true. We live with the dream that this person, this job, this financial agreement will make our lives better.

Our mates usually wind up being our sacrificial lambs because they usually can't win no matter what they do. Most of us are looking to have our emotional, physical, financial, and spiritual needs met by this one person whom we have deemed special. It's often an impossible task for those given the giant responsibility of making us happy. But no matter how many times we have been disillusioned in love, we will search until we find someone who appears to be our savior, who will fulfill our expectations. When our dreams are washed away once again in a pool of disappointment, we get bitter, angry, and resentful. Someone has to pay the price for this terrible lie we were told. When our partners fail to fulfill our expectations and the relationship falls apart, it is of course all their fault. Some of us refuse to see the wall of expectations that block us from seeing our other options.

Having awareness of our other choices is an extraordinary gift. But it comes with a price. The more awareness we have, the more difficult it is to lie to ourselves. When we don't take ownership of our wisdom, all the energy has to go somewhere, so it goes to the only place it knows—back into ourselves. If we fail to use the knowledge of our new insights to make choices to empower our lives, this knowledge turns on us, driving us deeper into our darkness.

If you insist on denying responsibility for your current reality, you will probably go deeper into denial, creating more justifications and rationalizations. When you don't want to give up your position or your circumstances, you have to create a big story to convince yourself and those around you why you cannot transcend your difficulties. You are unconsciously driven to create more drama to prove that your circumstances are different and beyond your control. You create a righteous reason why you need to maintain your battle, and it always seems to you that you are right and your enemy is wrong. You may even tell yourself that you have to battle to take care of yourself. Maybe you have a lawyer or a therapist adding fuel to the fire. Or better yet, maybe you say it's your karma, your mission, to teach your opponent a lesson. But maybe instead of teaching the lesson you would be better off learning the lesson that got you where you are today.

PARTNERSHIP WITH GOD

At every crossroads we are faced with making choices. Choose responsibility, and you get awareness. Choose love and compassion, and I promise you that, no matter how horrible your partner may be, things will change. With God as your partner, you cannot lose. God is a force that resides within you and within me. If you call on this force to support you in your choices, I promise you that it will. You may have to get down on your hands and knees every day, and some of you may even have to beg, but if you are committed to opening the door for the Divine to come in and help you, it will come.

You may be thinking at this point that this process is too difficult, that you can't do it. But if so, you're still thinking that you have to do it alone. You don't. Whenever I forget that I am being divinely guided, I read this message aloud: "Good morning, Debbie, this is God. I will be handling all your problems today, and I will not need your help. So relax and enjoy your day and know that I am with you always." Hearing this message reminds me that I can breathe deep and relax. We are always being divinely guided, though in times of struggle we tend to forget this. But it is in our power to choose on a daily basis to remember that we are not alone.

With God as your ally, you can choose to receive the lessons your partner is trying to teach you. You can choose to acknowledge all the gifts you have received from your ex. You can choose to use your divorce and to get as much value out of it as possible. And on a moment-by-moment basis, you can *choose* to look at life through the lens of gratitude

HEALING ACTION STEPS

1. Thinking back over the years of your marriage, list all the gifts you received from your ex-partner. Reflect on the things you have

learned about yourself as a result of being with him or her. What people and hobbies are in your life now that weren't there before you met? What weaknesses of your ex-spouse have you had to compensate for? How has this helped to build your character? Be thoughtful and honest, and spend some time compiling your list. Making your wedding gift list will transform your negative feelings into positive ones.

2. List all the things in your life for which you are grateful.

3. Each day acknowledge yourself for at least ten things you have done that you are proud of. Appreciate yourself for the little things that add up over time—getting out of bed, exercising, eating only one hot fudge sundae. . . . Do this in writing and out loud. Don't wait for a big accomplishment, like stopping smoking, to acknowledge yourself for your progress.

THE LAW OF

FORGIVENESS

Chapter Ten

THE PATH TO GOD

My grievances hide the light of the world.

THE COURSE IN MIRACLES

Once we have received the gifts of our marriage, we are ready to fully forgive our partner and ourselves. The Law of Forgiveness allows us to let go of our judgments and beliefs about what is right and what is wrong and find compassion for our entire self.

Compassion unfolds when we are in the presence of the perfection of the Universe, when we can experience ourselves in another. It comes with the great understanding of the difficulties and ambiguity of being a human being. Compassion is God's grace for those who ask. Once we have received compassion for ourselves, we are able to find compassion and forgiveness for our mate. Forgiveness is the key to releasing all the karmic cords that bind us to our partner in negative ways. Forgiveness is the essential component to freeing our hearts and liberating our souls. Forgiveness is the food that nourishes our bodies, our relationships, and our future.

The moment we forgive we free up all the energies that are blocking us from experiencing our divine nature in our everyday lives. We are spiritual beings who love to love, and when we deprive ourselves of the energy of love, we starve our souls. Forgiveness is the greatest act of courage because it breaks down the walls that we thought would protect us. But, in fact, there is no better protection than that which comes from complete and total love for all of mankind.

At a certain point after my divorce from Dan, I saw the possibility of my future. I began to accept that my life was in fact unfolding for my highest good. I surrendered my image of who I wanted Dan to be and accepted him for who he is. I relinquished my attachment to my life turning out as I had planned and allowed the possibility of having an extraordinary life guide my choices and daily behaviors. I began to take better care of my body. I nurtured a loving relationship with my son and cultivated new friendships. I deepened my spiritual practices and began to feel a more intimate connection with God. I listened more attentively to my inner voice and was open to receiving divine guidance. I made a choice to let go of the burdens of my past. I cleaned out my closets and got rid of everything that didn't serve me. I uncovered and released the toxic emotions that kept me bound to my resentments. I accepted responsibility for my feelings, took back my negative projections, and began to see how I had created the dramas that had limited me.

I looked diligently for the gifts that were hidden within every challenging circumstance that arose between Dan and me. Then I made the life-altering choice to reinterpret my experiences so that they empowered instead of disempowered me. Once my resentments had disappeared and my inner wounds had healed, I found gratitude. And with gratitude in my heart I was more than willing to forgive.

Now, standing in the doorway of forgiveness, I was able to look back and claim complete and total responsibility, not only for creating my marriage and separation but for how the rest of my life will turn out. Only then could I use the gifts of my marriage and appreciate the lessons that life had given me.

This wisdom enables us to surrender our resentments and reconnect with our divine nature. Our resentments are like a steel cord wrapped around our past, forever binding us to those we see as our opponents. We must become willing to step through the constricting door of blame into the unbounded world of forgiveness.

It's easy to be pissed off and embittered; in fact, it's quite natural. When I was going through my divorce, the thought of forgiving Dan made my stomach ache. The questions racing through my mind were: *Why should I be the one to forgive? Why should I give my ex-husband the grace of my loving energy?* I knew my mission was to rise above these impulses and raise the vibrational frequency of my thoughts. I knew my doubts and my fears kept me bolted to my ex-husband, and yet I still wanted to withhold my love and compassion. But by constantly praying to be released from my pain, I was blessed with the willingness to do the work that needed to be done before I could release Dan completely.

I knew that to have an emotional divorce as well as a physical divorce I had to forgive my own sins as well as those of my partner. Only then would I be free to interact with Dan in an empowering, compassionate way; only through forgiveness would I gain the control to act instead of react in challenging times. As difficult as forgiveness seemed, I knew it was the only way I could maintain a relationship with Dan for the next sixteen years. I didn't have the option of letting him go and never speaking to him again. We had joint custody of a young child, so for at least the next sixteen years I would need to interact with him. There was no way I was going to allow my grievances to overshadow my love for and commitment to my son, Beau. I knew what it was like to live with the knowledge of two parents' distaste for each other. I lived in that pain, and it terrified me to think that I could easily be capable of doing the same thing.

I prayed daily for God to please give me the courage and the knowledge to heal my pain, take away my anger, and help me find compassion for the father of my son. Even though I had never before been in this position, I knew that I had to arrive at a place of love for Dan. Even if I disagreed with him or disliked his behaviors, I knew that if I could focus on love and forgiveness, I would prevail in my efforts to free myself from the prison of my pain.

It took me almost two years to arrive at a place of authentic love that allowed me to be sincere in my efforts to have a supportive, respectful relationship with Dan. I wanted a relationship that would make Beau proud to have us as his parents. My yearning for harmony transcended what I wanted and didn't want. It transcended my small-ness and my righteous beliefs. It lifted me up and inspired me to step out of the grip of my negative feelings and step into a place of loving compassion.

AN INNOCENT HEART

Willingness is vital to the process of forgiveness. If we are *unwilling* to forgive, there is almost no chance that it will happen. Our willingness to forgive is essential to becoming whole again. Whole means that we are missing no parts, that we have access to all of our love, hope, and innate benevolence for all of mankind. All of us, no matter what our crimes, deserve a chance to mend our broken hearts. Imagine holding a sweet innocent child who is crying in your arms. Would you tell the child to let go of her pain or hold on to it? Would you tell her she is worthy of experiencing a whole, healed heart, or would you tell her to stay drenched in her pain?

The image of the child is a reminder of our innocence. An inno-cent heart never holds resentment or dwells in the pain of guilt. In the vision of our inner child we can allow our hearts to soften and surren-der to the gentle nature of forgiveness. No one deserves to carry the weight of a hardened heart. Pride prevents us from opening our hearts and forgiving. Spiritual pride is the act of withholding forgive-ness from ourselves. But no one deserves to carry the pounding pain of guilty feelings. Dr. Harold Bloomfield, author of *Surviving the Loss of a Loved One,* says, "Every day you don't forgive it's as if you are ingest-ing tiny bits of poison." This poison slowly robs us of our desired fu-ture. Whether we need forgiveness for ourselves or for others, it is imperative to give ourselves permission to participate in this sacred process.

Jake left Laura when their two sons were only toddlers. Laura worked hard to be a good mother and did everything in her power to make sure she could provide a safe, loving environment for her children. She spent years working through her feelings of abandonment and betrayal. She had come to a place of peace over the years, but there was always conflict with Jake about what the boys needed and how to raise them, and Jake, a bully, usually prevailed.

After ten years of being controlled by Jake's rules, Laura decided that she needed to fight for what she believed to be fair and asked Jake to pay her more child support for the boys. Jake had no intention of giving his ex-wife more money and instead decided that this was a good opportunity to fight for sole custody of the children.

Filled with anxiety, Laura went to mediation with Jake to try to work out their issues. Since the boys were already in high school, they were called in to help resolve the dispute. The boys decided that they were tired of going back and forth between both homes, and that since the school they attended was closer to their father's home, it would be easier for them to live at their dad's for a while.

After many weeks of uncertainty, the arbitrator called Jake and Laura into her office. In a quiet voice, the arbitrator began to speak. With her eyes focused on Laura's face, she said, "After considering all the evidence, the recommendation that I am giving the court is that Jake get sole custody of the two boys."

Laura sat there, unable to move. Her worst nightmare had come true. Tears stung her eyes, and pain filled her heart as she tried to digest the devastating news. Filling her body once again were all the same feelings she had felt so many years before when Jake walked out the door. Now, not only had he left, but he was taking the two people she loved most in the world. All she could think was that her family was being taken away from her. Jake had finally won the war they had fought for almost fifteen years. Now she would go home to her second husband, whom she loved, but Jake was going home with her heart in his hands.

Laura's pain was overwhelming. After weeks of sobbing, she knew she had only one choice—to heal. Gathering all of her inner strength, she began taking the necessary steps to heal her broken heart. Laura had adopted a prayer years earlier that helped her heal from her divorce, and now she would use it again. Several times a day Laura closed her eyes and visualized the sacred heart of compassion. After repeating the words "I surrender to the presence of God within me. Oh Lord, please come," she would find comfort. Laura knew that the sooner she accepted the decision of the court and her sons' choices, the sooner the pain would subside.

She desperately sought to take responsibility for co-creating her entire situation, and at the same time she knew that she needed to be kind to herself and to avoid adding to her bad feelings by beating herself up. Laura slowly began looking for the lesson that she was sure all these events were trying to teach her. With persistence, she uncovered a deeper understanding. She came to the great realization that her children came through her but that they didn't belong to her. Laura saw that her job was to support her kids in making good choices and to provide them with unconditional love. For fear of losing the love of her sons, she had held on tightly, but now she knew she had to let go because it was draining all of her energy.

Laura knew that to maintain a loving relationship with her sons she would have to forgive Jake and find compassion for all of his choices. In her mind she kept going back to the time when she loved Jake to see whether she could call forth those loving feelings again. It took time, persistence, and prayer for Laura to accept the fact that for at least the next couple of years her sons would be living with their father. She made peace with the fact that Jake had more money and more resources to offer them. He lived near their school of choice and shared many of the same interests, and the boys were at an age when they needed more of their dad.

It took Laura a long, hard year to transcend her loss and pain. But with God's help and her own determination, she made the best out of a bad situation. Her commitment to taking the higher road of forgiveness supported her in creating an even better relationship with her sons than when she had shared custody. The time they spent together now was precious. They planned outings, went for walks, and had intimate talks. They were all devoted to loving each other.

Forgiveness is the key that opens the door to our hearts. Forgiveness is there waiting for us the moment we are ready to surrender our will, claim responsibility for our circumstances, and trust that there is a plan for our lives beyond what we can see. When Laura lost custody of her sons, she couldn't even imagine that her loss would lead to something positive. But as a result of this difficult situation, they were able to create a deeper and more nurturing and loving relationship as a family.

When we embrace the perfection of this world, we're able to see the master plan of our lives beyond our ego's wishes. It is then that we experience a compassionate heart, a heart filled with deep understanding and compassion for all. We experience a heart that knows that things happen and people change for a reason, and, without a doubt, if we have the courage to take the higher road, we are rewarded with the gift of love, peace, and a contented heart.

Carole is a thirty-seven-year-old woman with one young daughter. After being divorced for over two years, she still spent a good part of every day bad-mouthing her partner and talking to lawyers. One morning Carole woke up sick to her stomach. The pain was intense, so she went to the doctor. After undergoing some tests, Carole was told that she had stomach cancer and would need surgery if she wanted to live. In those five minutes Carole's entire life was turned upside down. Suddenly she realized that her life might end. It terrified her to think that in less than a year she might be dead and that her time with her daughter would be over.

Carole went home and started praying. That evening she asked God to tell her what she needed to do to heal herself. The first thought that came to her mind was to drop the lawsuit against her ex-husband, John. Carole had been angry about a piece of real estate that she knew rightfully belonged to her. But now she knew that she needed to forget about the money she was owed and move on with her life and her healing. Before calling the doctors to schedule her surgery, she called her lawyer and instructed him to drop the lawsuit. She made a commitment never to fight with her ex-husband again.

Carole described to me the great relief she experienced that day. She knew the minute she hung up the phone with her lawyer that she would get well. Her resentments toward John had brought her only pain and suffering.

It took confronting a deadly disease for Carole to begin to live again. She now views winning and being right as the booby prize. Carole's only hope lay in surrender and forgiveness, and these became the new foundation for her life. Carole is now in full recovery and says that she has never felt better in her life. Her priorities have changed, and she appreciates every moment she's alive. Instead of filling her time with lawyers and legal documents, she now spends her time seeking love and peace of mind. Her daughter is doing great, and even her angry ex-husband often surprises her with a smile. Carole wants to live, but either way she finally feels good about herself. She is now free from suffering and able to enjoy the gifts of her life.

Forgiveness opened Carole's heart to love. It took a deadly diagnosis for her to see that she had only a small amount of time on this planet and that only she could choose how she was going to use it. Was she going to give her precious vital force to the person she felt had victimized her? Did she want to spend another waking hour or day talking about someone who had taken what was rightfully hers? Or did she want to surrender to the loss? He had something that was hers. She would have liked to have the property back, but it was certainly not worth another minute of her time, another phone call, or another breath of her life force. For the first time in Carole's life she realized just how precious each and every moment is. Every breath became a reason to rejoice.

For Carole, dropping the lawsuit against her ex-husband was the most important decision she ever made. She surrendered her outward battle for an inward gain. She traded her anger for love, her resentments for forgiveness. And her reward was her life. Today Carole realizes what a blessing her disease was. She doesn't have to struggle to turn the other cheek. It's her honor and relief to be 100 percent accountable for her life and the lessons that it brings.

YOU NEVER KNOW

Anna filed for divorce when she was forty-four years old. After years of loneliness, and with her children almost grown, Anna found the courage to leave her husband. She had caught Fred in a number of lies, and then one day found evidence of his affair with another woman. This violation of their marriage vows and of her trust was more than she could bear. So one morning, after Fred left for work, Anna packed up her clothes and some of her children's things and moved into an apartment of her own. Determined to escape her husband's control, she went to a lawyer and was advised of her rights if she were to pursue the divorce.

Fred did not take kindly to the breakup of his perfect little world. He called and pleaded with Anna to come home and bring back their children. She refused, and so the battle began. Fred had the money and the power to hire the best divorce attorney in town, and he set out to put enough pressure on Anna to drive her back into his home. At the end of two years and tens of thousands of dollars in legal bills, Anna had a child support order that barely paid for food and clothes.

Meanwhile, Anna had gone back to school to become a dental hygienist. She had a decent job, but for the next ten years Anna watched every dime; trying to make ends meet, she had little money left over for herself. She very much wanted her children to have everything the other children had. She worked hard to help her children through school.

Fred had taken a backseat in the raising of their children but remained distraught over the breakup of his marriage. Every year on their wedding anniversary he would send Anna a card asking for forgiveness. He wanted desperately to meet with Anna to discuss what had happened and to give her a gift. Anna refused. She had shut the door on that part of her life and had no intention of ever letting Fred anywhere near her again. At both their son's wedding and their daughter's college graduation, Fred approached Anna, asking for only a few minutes of her time. He said that he wanted to give her something, but she refused to give him the time of day.

Years went by, the children left home, the child support stopped, and Anna still had no more than just enough to get by in life. She was never able to do any of the extravagant things she had dreamed about, like attending the opera or traveling to foreign countries.

Then one day Anna received a call from her daughter informing her of Fred's death. He had died of a heart attack at age sixty-two. Anna was kind and caring to her children but suffered no remorse or sadness at the loss of Fred. Weeks later, when the will was being read, Anna's children showed up unexpectedly at her door. In their hands was a letter addressed to her from Fred. At first Anna refused to look at it, but at the insistence of her children she finally opened and read the following:

Dear Anna,

After many years of praying you would give me only five minutes to tell you how very sorry I am for all the pain I've caused you, I'm writing you this letter. I was young and a fool and have never gotten over the separation of our family. Watching the confused look in our children's eyes was actually the catalyst for understanding how very wrong I was to have violated our marriage vows. After promising I would take care of you till death do us part, I grieve at the loss of that opportunity. I would have given this money to you after the second year of our divorce, but you would never grant me even a moment to explain and I knew you would never have taken it. I thought that after years your heart would soften, but still, even at Gregory's wedding, you avoided my eyes. Watching you struggle, knowing I had something that could help make things easier for you, only compounded the pain in my own heart.

If you are reading this letter, I will know that you have outlived me and that it is too late for me to personally tell you how difficult my life has been since you left. I hope that now you will take this gift that I have longed to give you. It is rightfully yours. When we *were married, you'll remember, your parents gave us $10,000 to help us get started. Secretly I took that money from our account and invested it in a mutual fund. Even through our divorce I never disclosed this piece of information. Well, that stock is now worth over $150,000, and it's all yours. Now that I am gone, I hope that you take this money and buy yourself the beautiful clothes you deserve to wear. I hope you take a luxurious cruise to all the places you dreamed of traveling to, and I pray it gives you the security that I wished I would have provided for you. It's been a lonely life filled with regret. Maybe now you'll forgive me and I'll rest in peace knowing I finally have had my five minutes alone with you.*

Please forgive me now and take what is yours.

With love and regret,

Fred

The consequence of refusing to forgive is that we block ourselves from receiving unknown gifts. It is extremely difficult to feel our own self-worth when we are burdened with resentments. When we feel unworthy of happiness, we deny ourselves the everyday miracles that are available to each and every one of us. Inside our psyche, shame and resentment share a difficult dance. None of us ever dreamed of growing up to be an angry, resentful grudge-carrier. When we hold on to our resentments, an unknowing shame permeates our entire being and sabotages our feelings of worthiness. What we do to others we also do to ourselves. The resentments we hold on to so that we can punish others wind up punishing ourselves. Keeping a tight grip on the crimes of others leaves us with a burdened heart and diminishes our chances for receiving all the joy that life has to offer.

OPENING OUR HEARTS TO LIFE'S GIFTS

When we step through the door of forgiveness, a new reality emerges. Jeremiah Abrams, author of *Meeting the Shadow,* tells us: "The first step towards receiving all of life's gifts is to forgive everyone of everything and include yourself in the amnesty. If you can't forgive, it's because you are still harboring resentments which cause you to protect your heart. Harboring resentments seals off our hearts so we are unable to receive." To receive the gifts of the Universe we must open ourselves up to a place where we can hear the messages and the guidance of our higher self. It is then that we open ourselves up to receive all of the gifts that are waiting patiently for us to claim them.

This is the time to claim what is rightfully yours. Don't allow your resentments to keep you stuck in the pain of your past. Don't give up your life to someone who has disappointed and hurt you. Don't let your divorce stop you from claiming the love you deserve and the life you desire.

"Nobody has the right to wreck your day, let alone your life. And guess what? Nobody does, you do," says Gary Fenchuk, author of *Timeless Wisdom.* We are each accountable for our own happiness. No one can take it away from us. We give our power away, we give parts of ourselves away, and then we get angry when our partners leave, taking away what we gave them.

Forgiveness is the shortest route to God. We begin this journey by making a list of everything we need to be forgiven for and all that we want to forgive in our partners. As an example, here is Robin's forgiveness list:

I FORGIVE MYSELF FOR...

I forgive myself for not communicating in a responsible way.

I forgive myself for my anger and for abusing Richard with my emotions.

I forgive myself for lying to Richard in saying that money wasn't important to me.

I forgive myself for my dissatisfaction.

I forgive myself for marrying someone who wasn't a professional.

I forgive myself for marrying a man who was insecure.

I forgive myself for not listening to Richard.

I forgive myself for fighting so much.

I forgive myself for not trusting my instincts.

I forgive myself for physically hurting Richard.

I forgive myself for allowing my parents to influence my feelings about my husband.

I FORGIVE MY PARTNER FOR . . .

I forgive Richard for not being able to fulfill my desire for beautiful things.

I forgive Richard for not buying me my dream home.

I forgive Richard for his arrogance.

I forgive Richard for not wanting to hang out with my family.

I forgive Richard for not wanting to spend more time traveling, going to the theater, or window-shopping.

I forgive Richard for not spending more time with my friends.

I forgive Richard for being so antisocial.

I forgive Richard for his opinions.

I forgive Richard for being mean to my family and friends.

I forgive Richard for not being successful.

I forgive Richard for not providing me with financial security.

Robin and Richard did their forgiveness lists separately, but as you'll see, there are many similarities between them. Both had held resentments that reflected their common issues. Richard's list looked like this:

I FORGIVE MY PARTNER FOR . . .

I forgive Robin for raging at me.

I forgive Robin for dancing sexually suggestively at parties.

I forgive Robin for sucking up to rich people.

I forgive Robin for not taking care of her possessions.

I forgive Robin for getting traffic tickets, getting into accidents, and having our car insurance canceled.

I forgive Robin for foolishly wasting money.

I forgive Robin for not taking my good advice.

I forgive Robin for being grandiose.

I forgive Robin for making me socialize with people who are boring.

I forgive Robin for then calling me antisocial.

I FORGIVE MYSELF FOR . . .

I forgive myself for disliking Robin's parents.

I forgive myself for not wanting to socialize with her friends.

I forgive myself for not giving her money.

I forgive myself for not buying her the gifts she requested.

I forgive myself for getting angry with her.

I forgive myself for getting ill.

I forgive myself for withholding sex and affection.

I forgive myself for being a workaholic.

Once we make our forgiveness list, for both ourselves and our partner, we are ready to ask divine grace to intervene and take away our anger, sadness, and regrets.

After three years of struggling to save their marriage, Pauline and Isaac decided finally to cut the ties. Pauline had endured years of emotional pain trying to make herself better in order to hold on to a hopeless situation. Isaac was always standing with one foot out the door, and Pauline was now ready to say her final good-bye. Pauline's therapist and I worked together to help her create a divorce ritual that would signify their separation. I suggested that she write a letter to Isaac to say whatever was left unexpressed in her heart. This is her letter:

Dear Isaac,

Odd to write this to you, because I thought I had written my last letter to you ages ago. I need to do this for myself, and I hope it will help you to understand what I am truly feeling.

We have had many wonderful times together. At this time I am safe knowing that I love you, and just as safe saying that I am not in love with you. You were my best friend, and I couldn't have made this journey without you. I miss you terribly. It is so hard some days to not have you to talk to. I wonder if you are well, if you are happy.

I want to thank you for standing up for me when no one else would. You were there. I want to thank you for listening to my rantings and ravings for years. Even though they scared you at times, you stayed. Thank you. You and I were a great team. We knew in many ways how to balance each other. When I was down, you believed in me. When you were down, you let me stand there to support you. What an honor. Thank you. I have moved mountains within, and the time has come to thank and acknowledge you for being a large part of the fuel. Please forgive me for any words that I said that hurt you, for any behavior that scarred you. I release you from any guilt you might be feeling. You did not injure me. Because of you I have come to know myself deeply. It is time for me to go on with my life. I will never forget you.

Love,
Pauline

Pauline wrote this letter for herself. She needed to say good-bye to create a ritual of completion. It was not necessary for her to send it. The release she needed came from writing the words and allowing herself to feel her deepest emotions without censoring herself. Now it was time for her to extend the same forgiveness to herself. I suggested that Pauline write a letter of forgiveness to herself:

Dear Pauline,

I can't think of one human I know who is tougher on herself than you. You've criticized and chastised yourself and made yourself feel inferior. You've deprived yourself of great happiness and incredible loving relationships. You've taken yourself away from family and friends. Your self-loathing drove you to the point that you have given everything you have away, financially as well as emotionally, just to get a morsel of love.

If I knew someone who had been treated so harshly, it never would have continued. I would have removed that person from such abuse, and helped guide them truly away from you. If I had known, I would have stopped your inner violence a long, long time ago.

I have only recently come to understand what intense and powerful crimes those acts against yourself were. I am so sorry, Pauline, that I didn't see them sooner. To have been so close to it all and not to have seen it—how scary.

We really don't see the violence and destruction when it's not only right next door but within our very selves.

You are in this moment, here standing in all your glory, apologizing to yourself. You did not deserve to be so battered, so beaten up, so deprived of being loved. You deserved to be loved, honored, respected, and nourished. I am so sorry to have taken all those things away from you. You deserve better.

I thank you for loving yourself enough to fight for your very rights, because you deserve them. You are right, God is a loving being. He does not want you to suffer, he wants you to love, be loved, and feel love. Thank you for letting me finally, after a harsh, violent journey, still be able to see that.

Please forgive me. I love you.
Pauline

Forgiveness of our partners *and* ourselves is mandatory to a conscious divorce. Only through our willingness to take responsibility for and ownership of our resentments can we heal. Practicing forgiveness is a way of life. We have to close our eyes daily and pray to forgive everyone who has harmed us. It doesn't happen overnight, and we must do the internal work first before we even try to find forgiveness.

You can't will forgiveness—it is part of a process. You have to feel the hurt that caused your wound and diffuse the anger that arose to protect the hurt. Forgiveness is the hallway between your past and your future. If you choose to hold on to your anger and resentments, you will continue living a life from your past. What you can always expect when you live a life from your past is more of the same. But if you dare to walk through the door of forgiveness, you will step into a new room and a new reality. You will create a life filled with love, compassion, and passion for living. You'll be ready to create a future based on what you want instead of one created by what you don't want.

HEALING ACTION STEPS

1. Make a list of all the behaviors and incidents for which you want to be forgiven. Write another list of all the behaviors for which you want to forgive your partner.

2. After writing your list, say a prayer asking for forgiveness for yourself and your partner. Then put your list in a sealed envelope on your altar next to a seven-day candle. Light this candle every day with the intention of becoming free from your resentments by the end of the seventh day.

3. List all the people with whom you have grievances and write down what you need to forgive them for. Ask God to support you in granting them complete and total amnesty.

THE LAW OF

CREATION

~ Chapter Eleven ~

RECLAIMING YOUR DIVINE LIGHT

It takes both rain and sunshine to make a rainbow.

ANONYMOUS

The Law of Creation guides us to design a new future that is grounded in divine truth. Rather than being trapped in the limited reality of our smallest thought, we can now stand in the limitless freedom of our biggest dream. Having embraced our darkest qualities, it is now time to reclaim our light, our loving, compassionate, creative self. Only when we embrace our darkness and our light equally do we have access to our entire self. And only when we have access to all of who we are can we align with the destiny of our higher selves. When we are dancing in the arms of our soul's purpose, each of us naturally expresses the precious gifts that we hold.

The Law of Creation tells us that forgiveness breaks all the cords that have kept us tied to the past. When I stepped into the freedom of forgiveness, my life took on a different texture. The days of being a slave to the bitter dialogue that had occupied my mind were gone. A new kind of freedom began to emerge inside of me that I had longed to experience. None of my external circumstances had changed, and yet everything looked entirely different. An ease permeated every cell of my being. I knew inside that I was going to be okay and I could finally go on with my life. I had come to realize that my worries and

189

doubts were all a result of my limiting beliefs. A new truth had finally emerged: I was safe in the world.

I could now let go of the heavy armor that I had constructed to protect myself from my alleged opponent. With the release of that armor, the dark, heavy cloud that had loomed over me lifted, and what appeared in its place was love and appreciation for just how lucky I was to be born on this earth. My constant frown was replaced by a smile, and my heavy mood was transformed into a joyous appreciation for being a child of God.

Nothing could have prepared me for the tremendous loss and darkness I went through to heal myself from my separation from Dan. Day after day I questioned my choices. Even when I was perfectly clear that I had made the right decisions, a moment later that certainty would fade, replaced by self-doubt.

But I was standing in a new place, a new land, looking around at an earth I had never seen before. This new earth was not the dry, hard ground I had previously known, but rather a rich, moist soil filled with limitless possibilities. I realized that the purpose of my long and painful journey was to till the soil of my consciousness. I needed to get rid of the weeds and other parasites that had been sucking the essential nutrients out of my life force. And now that I had completed this process, I was standing on rich, fertile ground. My consciousness had been cleansed, and I was ready to plant the seeds of my desires and receive the gifts that life wanted to bring to me.

I stood marveling at the realization that where I stood was exactly where I was supposed to be and that every upset, disappointment, and unfilled expectation had brought me to this sacred moment.

It was both thrilling and scary because I had never known myself to be this way before. Something so fundamental to my old self had changed that now I would have the opportunity to meet myself anew. I had finally broken free from the constricting walls of my emotional cocoon. Freeing myself of my internal and external struggles reminded me of a poignant story. A man is walking along when he comes across a caterpillar nestled in its cocoon. Curious, he picks it up and brings it to his home so that he can watch it emerge into a beautiful butterfly.

Days later a small opening appears, and for several hours the caterpillar struggles but can't seem to force its body past a certain point.

Deciding that something is wrong, the man takes out a pair of scissors and snips the remaining bit of cocoon. Moments later the butterfly emerges easily, its body large and swollen. Its tiny wings are small and shriveled. The man sits close by expecting that in a few hours the wings will spread out in their natural beauty, but they do not. Instead of developing into a creature free to fly, the butterfly spends its life dragging around a swollen body and shriveled wings.

The butterfly's struggle to escape the constricting cocoon and pass through the tiny opening is God's way of forcing fluid from its body into its wings. The man's "merciful" snip was, in reality, cruel. When we are suffering and trying to move through our pain, we wish that someone could come along and save us, but in truth it is this struggle that gives us what we need to develop into the magnificent creatures we were born to be. During my divorce it became apparent to me that everything was as it should be and that I had to go through every struggle, large and small, to arrive at a place where I could spread my divine wings and fly.

There hasn't been a day since I emerged into the person I have become that I haven't thanked God for all that I am and all that I have. I am rich beyond measure because I am filled with an unshakable knowledge that there is a God and that this all-loving, compassionate being does love me. I now stand grounded in the truth that we are all born with a unique imprint unlike that of anyone else in the entire Universe. Each of us, without exception, has a special purpose and place on this earth.

No one can do what you can do in the exact way that you can do it. Every fingerprint is different because each one of us is unique. Each of our souls is imprinted with an individual map that guides us to the unique circumstances that will best support us in manifesting the glory of God on this earth. You matter. What you do, how you act, and the choices you make, all of it matters. You are an important part of humanity, and a valuable piece of this earth. If you knew how special you are, you would be shouting out your window in joy.

One of my son's kindergarten teachers explained it beautifully. On the first day of school Mrs. Knight handed all the children who walked into class a piece of a puzzle with a number on it. As she called up each student by number, the child brought his or her piece of the puzzle to her and Mrs. Knight placed it in the correct position inside the cardboard frame that held the puzzle together. There were twenty children and twenty pieces of the puzzle. When Mrs. Knight finally called number 20, the entire picture on the puzzle was filled in except for one missing piece: the little boy who would have carried number 19 was missing from class that day, and to see the full beauty of the picture the class needed him. This was how Mrs. Knight illustrated to the children how important each of them was to complete the whole.

I sat there with tears in my eyes, thinking about the vital contribution that each and every one of us makes to the whole of humanity. Each of us contributes an important piece that completes the picture of life. When we are stuck in the past, it is almost impossible to claim our piece of the puzzle and put it where it was designed to go. And when we choose to accept our life's mission, we contribute a unique piece of this amazing earth puzzle.

You and I have free will. We have the right to choose whether we will contribute our unique piece to the puzzle of the Universe or walk away from it. I know with certainty that if you do the work to heal yourself at the deepest level, you will fall in love with the person you become. Not only will you feel worthy of expressing your unique gifts, but you will feel impassioned to fulfill your role here on earth. Having a spiritual divorce can support you in discovering and contributing your unique piece of the puzzle.

Like most of us, I have longed to do something good in the world since I was a small child. Even though I had that desire, I always had circumstances, reasons, and excuses that prevented me from realizing my dreams. My divorce gave me the final push through the cocoon of my own insecurities. I was now responsible for myself and my young son, so I had to spread my wings if I was going to fly.

If somebody had snipped my cocoon by saving me from that pain, if another man had come along to rescue me, if I had gotten enough money out of my divorce to live comfortably for many years, I never would have emerged from the cocoon of my own limiting beliefs. If I had gotten what my small self wanted—financial and emotional security—I would never have received the last push and experienced the strength of my full potential. My divorce was the catalyst that launched me into sharing my gifts with the world.

Making the commitment to share my gifts with the world is the greatest accomplishment of my life. The rewards outweigh the risks a hundred to one. Finally, after all the years of pain and suffering, it feels so good to claim my piece. It feels so right to fit in and do what my soul longs to do. Trading my will for God's will was the best investment I ever made. It took many years while I resisted and fought, screaming and kicking, all because my ego wanted so desperately to be right and to win. But I can tell you now, only in hindsight, that the way of my ego has been wrong most of the time. As hard as I tried to win, I lost most of the major battles I ever fought. I lost in love, I lost for years in my struggle to overcome drug addiction, I lost in business, and I lost with friends. But all my losses were necessary before I could finally surrender to a place where I don't mind losing anymore. Surrendering is a blessing, and today I would rather be happy than right. I would rather lose many small battles but win the war. It turned out that the war I was waging was not with the world but within myself. The peace treaty needed was between my ego and my soul.

The Universe is always teaching and guiding us through the challenges of our lives. Each change of life brings us another opportunity to align with our soul, that part of us connected to all that is and all that will ever be. When we align with our soul, our hearts guide us to make the highest evolutionary choices at every moment.

ALIGNING WITH OUR SOULS

You may be asking, "How can I tell the difference between my ego and my soul?" It's actually quite simple. Your ego always knows, and your soul doesn't need to know. Your ego lives in fear, and your soul lives in trust. Your ego resists when things aren't going its way, and your soul surrenders, trusting that the river of life is taking you exactly where you need to go. Your ego dwells in the past, and your soul lives in the present, with the profound knowledge that this moment is all there is. Your ego will do anything to be right, and your soul knows that it will gain strength, knowledge, and wisdom from all the times it is wrong. Your ego is serious, and your soul is light and joyful. Your ego blames, and your soul takes complete responsibility for co-creating every circumstance. Your ego stands in judgment, and your soul comforts you with compassion.

Most of us get caught in the dilemma of deciding which path to follow. There is a comforting familiarity to following the path of our ego. It tricks us into believing that we will be safe if we stay where we are. Even if we've gotten into trouble listening to the voice of our ego, at least it's a companion we can count on. But to step into the world beyond our ego we must surrender to the path of the Universe. We must follow the universal map for our lives and trust that when we get to the place that has been carved out especially for us, we will get what we need and secure the satisfaction we've been looking for.

I am writing this book today because that is what my soul guided me to do. Nowhere in my ego's plan for my life was there a book called *Spiritual Divorce*. But one day, while going through a very rough time, I got quiet in a meditation and asked God, "Why is this happening? What is the lesson I am supposed to learn from this? How will this experience help me to become a better person?" The answer came effortlessly. I knew I would one day use my experience to help others. It was then that I realized that the divorce of my parents and now my own divorce had given me the exact experiences necessary to fulfill this commitment.

It would be four years after the first seed of this book was planted in my consciousness before I finally wrote the first page. Why the delay? Writing a divorce book did not fit into my image of what I should be doing. But now that I am nearing the end of this miraculous process of birthing a book, I can honestly tell you that I have never felt better or stronger. Never before have I felt so in tune with the Universe, and nothing has changed the direction of my life so much.

SURRENDERING TO GOD'S PLAN

God's plan does not always look the way we think it should. In fact, most people who have settled into the comfort of their soul's work, if asked, would probably say that they never knew where they were going until they arrived. The educator and author Joseph Campbell tells us, "You have got to let go of the life you have planned to live the life that is waiting for you."

To follow the path of our souls we must be willing to give up our image of ourselves and surrender into the unknown and unfamiliar. We must take the risk of giving up all that we know. The core beliefs that drove us to our present circumstances will remain intact until we dismantle them. Charles Dubios says, "The important thing is to be able at any moment to sacrifice what you are for what you can become."

The only way I can do this is to step outside my ego's ideal of who I am. My ego is attached to who I think I am. My soul knows that I am everything. My soul knows that I am more than my body, my experiences, or my credentials, and as long as I bring forth the very best that is within me, I will revel in the glory of a satisfied and fulfilled life.

EMBRACING YOUR LIGHT

To discover and express your highest possibility you must embrace your light just as you have embraced your darkness. Your light shadow is the opposite of your dark shadow, and claiming it represents the next step in your personal evolution.

While your dark shadow is the person you would rather not be, your light shadow is represented in the people who inspire you. We can find our disowned positive qualities by looking outside ourselves at those we admire, those we love, and those whom we would like to emulate. When you look outside, you can see yourself in the mirror image of others. Just as we have given so much of our darkness away, we have also hidden that much of our light. We hid our light out of fear of being too bold, dreaming too loudly or out of a belief that we don't deserve to express all our greatness.

You must remember, however, that you are everything—there is nothing you see outside yourself that isn't you.

Having understood the meaning of wholeness, I began the exciting journey of looking for myself in others. Whenever I was affected by somebody's presence in a positive way, if I felt joy, excitement, or even a twinge of envy, I would identify the specific qualities in the other person that were inspiring to me. I made a list of three people who demonstrated qualities I wanted to bring forth in myself. I perceived my sister Arielle as hardworking, inspiring, and focused. I loved the writings of Emmett Fox, who I found to be wise, understanding, and sincere. And when I sat in the presence of Amachi, a spiritual teacher believed by many to be a living saint, I was moved by her compassion, selfless service, and philanthropic endeavors.

Before me was an inspiring list of qualities that were all undiscovered parts of myself waiting to be born. They were the particular qualities I needed to see. They caught my eye like shiny jewels. I came to understand that these positive qualities that I recognized in others were polished versions of the same qualities that lay in rough form within me. My sister's focus was highly refined. You could see it clearly in the way she lived her life. My own focus was like a diamond in the rough that needed to be mined and polished. All of what I admired in other people were parts of me waiting to be brought forth from my unconscious. All of these people were my mirrors showing me to myself, and if I didn't claim these essential aspects of who I am, they would remain untouched.

Searching for my hidden jewels became an exciting adventure because every time I found something in someone else that I loved, I could claim another part of myself. I knew that if I chose to be bold and embrace the qualities I admired, I would forever be in the presence of my own magnificence.

The qualities I perceived in others gave me a clearer picture of what I am capable of, at my highest expression. I closed my eyes to breathe in the possibility that each and every trait I loved in others was simply a part of me. If I wanted to embody these qualities in myself—hardworking, inspiring, focused, wise, understanding, heartfelt, compassionate, philanthropic, and selfless—all it would take is awareness and a little work.

When I began this examination of my life, I didn't think I had any of these qualities. Yet, for unseen reasons, I yearned to manifest them. Later I discovered that the qualities being sparked within me were the secret to igniting my potential. Shining directly into my soul through my perceptions of others was all that I had ever desired to be, and now that I had discovered this, all I had to do was claim them as mine.

Inspired, I gathered all the qualities that resonated with my highest vision of myself. I began to make a list of the actions I could take to cultivate and elicit these qualities in myself. I started by looking for my understanding self. I closed my eyes and asked, *How can I be more understanding of others?* My first thought was that I could start by being more considerate of other people's point of view. I wrote down all the actions I could take that would be consistent with what I envisioned an understanding person would do. Similarly, if I wanted to be more compassionate, all I had to do was practice walking in another's shoes to bring forth the compassion that was dormant within me.

The thought of being philanthropic and helping thousands of people less fortunate than myself excited me. I began to donate money to causes that touched me, and even though my donations were small, making them helped me to own the philanthropic aspect of myself. With my eyes closed, I asked myself, *What would I be doing if I were more focused?* The answer was simple: *I would have to stop dwelling in the negativity of my past and put all my attention on a plan for my future.* That was all I needed to hear to begin gathering support for what would turn out to be the writing of my first book.

Finding all these aspects within myself was much easier than I ever expected. It took only the willingness to hold the vision of my most extraordinary self.

TAKING BACK WHAT IS OURS

Now it was time to deepen my search and make sure that my partner was not leaving the relationship with any parts of me. Just as we project negative aspects of ourselves onto our partners, we also project our light. For most of us when we fall in love it is because we are seeing our disowned light in someone else. We see in our mates a part of ourselves that is hidden, and then the chase begins to capture what we believe will make us whole.

When I met Dan, I was excited by his brilliant mind and the way he articulated his thoughts. I was inspired by his thirst for transformation. And I was touched by his sensitivity to people's pain. To take back my light shadow, I had to make sure that I was embracing my brilliance, my sensitivity, and the part of me that seeks transformation. If I thought that he had a talent or possessed a quality that I didn't have, that was a signal telling me that I hadn't embraced that quality within myself.

Immediately I knew that I had projected my own brilliance onto Dan because I had always had issues about not being smart enough. So of course I had been attracted to a man who went to an Ivy League school, was highly credentialed, and had attained many academic awards. What I needed to realize was that I was blessed not with Dan's kind of brilliance but with my own kind. Dan was school-smart, and I was street-smart. Both are highly valuable traits. To reclaim the brilliance I had transferred onto Dan I needed to recognize and embrace the ways in which I expressed my own unique brilliance. After taking back my projections, I could see the many gifts that my brilliance offered. Each of us expresses the same qualities in different ways. But to return to our own authentic state of emotional wholeness we must claim what we see in others as our own qualities.

You must take the time to see what you were attracted to in your partner and to reclaim any aspects you have given away, consciously or unconsciously. Maybe your husband is walking away with your success or your stature in life. Maybe your wife is leaving with your kindness and compassion. Did you give your husband your sexiness and now fear that you won't have access to it if he leaves? Is your wife walking out the door with the part of you that is powerful and strong? You gave these parts of yourself away, and now it's time to take them back. When you've given your light shadow away and your partner is holding parts of you, it's impossible to fully let him or her go.

It's not until we can embrace both our light and dark sides—all of our positive traits and all of our negative traits—that we can truly experience the feeling of emotional wholeness. As long as either side is out of balance, we continue to get trapped in the world of separatism. We are caught in the noisy internal dialogue that says, *I am not that!*

Embracing your positive traits is a daily discipline that requires dedication and trust. The path to wholeness calls you to own and embrace every quality on the planet. Now is the time for you to embrace your magnificence.

HEALING ACTION STEPS

1. List three people you admire and identify three qualities in each of them that you would like to emulate. Close your eyes and identify where or when in your life you've displayed each quality. What behaviors and actions would bring these qualities more fully into your life?

2. Identify the qualities in your partner that initially attracted you. Think about what you fell in love with or what you are still yearning for. Even if you're angry, it's important to uncover the qualities in your partner that you love or admire.

Chapter Twelve

AN EXTRAORDINARY
LIFE

And the day came when the risk to remain closed in a bud
became more painful than the risk it took to blossom.

ANAÏS NIN

The Law of Creation invites us to experience an innocent heart
filled with love and excitement for life. It is often said that we
need to "open our hearts," but in truth our hearts are always open. We
just don't have access to them because we keep them so well guarded.

This is the time to let go of your armor, your defenses, and your
excuses and to open up to the wisdom of the heart. People may tell you
to fight, to protect yourself, but fighting will only keep you trapped in
a small world. To create a future grounded in divine truth you must
step out of the world you are living in. Without your armor, you are
free to step into new, uncharted territories where you are graced with
unlimited access to your divine nature. This is a vital time: you get to
choose what kind of person you want to be. Do you want to live an ordinary life, or do you want to reach out into new horizons and create
an extraordinary life?

A few months after my divorce was final I woke up one morning
wondering what it would take to create an extraordinary life, one that
was sourced by my divine light. I was afraid that after forty years of

heading in one direction, I didn't have what it took to change my path and create the life of my dreams. I kept asking myself, *How can I create a life that isn't just more of the same?* I knew I couldn't go back to the way things were, to the way I was, and yet I wasn't sure how to break out of the shell of my past. Then, like an angel, my girlfriend Danielle arrived, handing me a beautiful children's story about an extraordinary crab that would be the inspiration for my new direction.

Grasper, whose story was written and illustrated by Paul Owen Lewis, lives near the rocks with many other crabs. They spend their days scavenging for bits of food and staying close to home. One day something peculiar happens to Grasper. He starts to feel quite strange, as if he no longer fits inside his body. Suddenly everything seems different. Then Grasper realizes that his shell has split: instead of being on him, it is lying on the ground next to him. Grasper is shocked to see before him a perfect silhouette of his crab body—arms, legs, eyes, and all.

It isn't long before the other members of Grasper's tight-knit community of crabs have gathered in a circle around him. They explain to Grasper that his shell has just molted, and they caution him that weird things will begin to happen if he isn't careful. They tell Grasper that the period of time before his new shell hardens is very dangerous, and they warn him not to listen to the voices that will soon be filling his head. They tell him that he may want to explore places he's never seen before and may even be inclined to look beyond the rocks where they live.

Grasper hears what all the frightened crabs are telling him, but instead of listening he begins to follow his urge to explore the world outside of what he knows. Trusting his feelings, Grasper crawls out from behind the rocks where he has safely spent all of his life and ventures into new, unknown territory. All the while his friends are screaming, "Stop, Grasper! It's not safe out there!"

When Grasper reaches the top, he can't believe what he sees. Everything is colorful and bright. There are large, beautiful fish and lots of food to eat. It's a magical sight unlike any he has ever seen, and Grasper is filled with excitement. Then, coming out from behind a rock,

Grasper comes face to face with a giant crab. It is the biggest crab Grasper has ever seen. When he asks the crab how he got so large, the crab explains to Grasper that the same thing will happen to him if he continues to grow and molt. But Grasper can't believe this explanation because all the crabs he knows are as small as himself. The giant crab explains to Grasper that a crab grows only as large as the world he lives in, and as big as the heart inside him. He says, "You must have a big heart to live in a big world."

Grasper is perplexed. He's been taught that to be safe in the world he must have a hard shell and a hard heart. But now he sees that if he wants to reach his full potential and grow into a giant crab, he will have to expand his horizons. Grasper will have to allow his heart to stay soft, for a hard heart can't grow.

Grasper is now faced with the biggest decision of his life. His past is telling him that it would be safer to harden his heart and return to his familiar little home by the rocks. But the process of molting and softening has changed Grasper. He no longer wants just to survive. He longs to break free from the small world he has lived in and to swim out into the vast ocean to see what it has in store.

Like Grasper, when we are molting, we question who we are, where we belong, and what we are truly capable of. We literally shed our skins during times of intense emotional pain. We molt away our previous identities. And yet it is only in the presence of this profound vulnerability that we gain the clarity and freedom to step out of the predictable shell of our past and make new decisions about how we want to live our lives. The choice is ours. We can choose to continue to live in a small world made up of blame, victimization, toxic emotions, and separatism, or we can step into a new world filled with acceptance, responsibility, connectedness, and peace of mind. To live in this new world we must surrender all the armor that protects our soft hearts.

It is scary to let go and take risks. But even if you try and fail, at least you are living fully. If you remain stuck in the pain of a relationship that is over, a part of you will die. Slowly all of your internal juices that source your vitality and enthusiasm for life will dry up.

Pain is a spiritual wake-up call showing you that there are oceans you have not yet explored. Step beyond the world you know. Reach for heights that you never thought possible. Go to places you have deemed off limits. This is the time to take off the shell of your past and step into the rich possibilities of your future. God does not give us dreams that we cannot fulfill. If you want to do something great with your life—whether it's to fall madly in love, become a teacher, be a great parent—if you aspire to do something beyond what you are doing now, this is the time to begin. Trust yourself. Notice the people in the world whom you envy and ask, *What do they have that I want? What are they doing that I want to be doing?*

When I was going through my divorce, the people who inspired me were meditating and had a rich spiritual life. So I knew that was what I needed to do. When I looked at women who were doing yoga, I admired the softness and flexibility of their bodies, so I began to do yoga. Years ago, when I discovered that I admired many authors, I began to take writing classes. I didn't know where these choices would lead me, but I did know this: if I continued making the same choices I had been making, I would end up right where I was. A Chinese proverb says it well: "If we don't change our direction, we are likely to end up where we are headed." If you want to arrive at a new destination, begin by taking new actions.

CHANGING THE DIRECTION OF YOUR LIFE

Taking risks is scary, but it is not as scary as standing still for twenty years. How many people do you know who are still caught up in doing the same thing, with the same people, day after day, and talking about "one day" when they find their pot of gold? Ordinary people wait for the pot of gold to show up, and extraordinary people go out and mine their gold. Extraordinary people hold themselves accountable for their choices, their actions, and their destination. They don't wait for "one day" because that day is today.

I lecture around the country, and in the past four years I have heard thousands of horror stories about emotional and physical abuse, deceit, and rage. My heart feels for each and every person who has suffered. But I know without a shadow of a doubt, without exception, that if you use this pain, if you choose to get the most out of it, you will receive blessings as deep and as rich as the hurts themselves. I know the pain of loss, of confusion, of loneliness, and of a broken heart. And I also know that unless you use that pain to heal yourself, you will use it to destroy yourself. Pain is the alarm that reminds you that you have separated yourself from your divine nature.

It has been said that the difference between an ordinary life and an extraordinary life is only the intention, the commitment that you make to yourself and to the Universe. An extraordinary person is an ordinary person doing extra-ordinary things.

Standing at the gateway to the life I desired, I was faced with this choice. I had committed myself to using my divorce as a catalyst for change, and there could be no bigger transformation than to turn this bad situation into a blessing in disguise. I knew that in order to grow to the heights I aspired to, I would have to reexamine all of my behaviors and actions. I began dwelling on these questions: *What would I do if I were extraordinary? How would I live? How would I speak? How could I have an extraordinary relationship with my ex-husband?* It was apparent that the choice was mine. I wanted to know how extraordinary people thought and what commitments guided their choices and actions. And I wanted to know how I, Debbie Ford, an ordinary woman, could lead an extraordinary life.

IF YOU WERE AN ANGEL

As life would have it, the Universe immediately gave me an opportunity to test my commitment and my desire. One day when I was in the midst of an upsetting time with Dan, my sister, Arielle, came over to visit me. Dan had wanted to make a change in his scheduled time with Beau. For no apparent reason, his effort to change the schedule triggered an emotional reaction in me, showing me that I was still carrying resentment from other times when Dan had made schedule changes.

Seeing that I was about to explode, Arielle asked me to close my eyes and take some deep breaths. She told me she had a very important question to ask me. After I had settled down a little, Arielle asked, "Debbie, if you were an angel what would you do in this situation?" My first thought was, *But I am not an angel!* I knew she was trying to trick me into seeing the situation from a different perspective, and I decided to let her give it her best shot.

So I considered that I was a beautiful angel flying around the room. As soon as I surrendered to this image, I had the sense that if I were an angel I would graciously give in to Dan's request. I certainly would not allow myself to get upset over a change in the schedule. If I were an angel, I wouldn't drag my resentments into the present, and I certainly wouldn't allow anyone outside of myself to disturb my peace of mind. It literally took only a minute to see that there were other options and other choices. All of them had validity, so I asked myself, *Which option will bring me peace? Which viewpoint will empower my relationship with Dan? Which one would make me the kind of woman I want to be?*

It was obvious to me that if I wanted to have an extraordinary relationship with Dan, I would have to make a series of extraordinary choices. And the time to make a new choice was now. Seeing my life through the eyes of an angel, a more evolved version of myself, shifted me into a more open state of mind in which I could choose from a higher place. The right decision was never in doubt once I looked at the situation from this higher ground. I could choose from the noisy, discontented, always right part of myself or from the loving, contented, peaceful part of myself. The choice was clearly mine. "By shifting your viewpoint to the angelic perspective, you become an Earth angel," writes Dr. Doreen Virtue, author of *Divine Guidance.* "Holding an elevated viewpoint sparks a miraculous healing in all of your relationships. Conflict drops away, revealing the clean and new truth about everyone and everything."

Viewing my life through angelic eyes added another missing piece to my healing process. From that day forward I committed myself to taking the time to view my choices and my actions through the eyes of an angel. After my ego finally surrendered to the fact that I wasn't going to let it make the choices, my internal conflict subsided.

And now I want to tell you the most extraordinary part of this entire process. After months of choosing from this higher place, I began to see that Dan was treating me differently. It almost seemed like he was treating me like an angel.

MAKING A VOW

It is essential to create a vision of your future relationship with your ex. If you're reading this book, I am assuming that you have broken or will be breaking your marriage vows. Now is the perfect time to create a new vow for your divorce. A divorce vow is a statement that describes your commitment to your relationship. The statement should be composed with thought and care, and it should nurture your commitment to a Spiritual Divorce. Like a mission statement, it is a reference point for your actions and commitments. A divorce vow serves as a springboard into your new reality.

When I forgave Dan, I wanted to create a reminder for myself of my highest intentions for our continuing relationship. Whenever I get upset or feel angry or stuck, I can read what I wrote and go back to the reality of forgiveness. If I am in a bad mood and Dan asks me to do him a favor like picking Beau up or changing weekends at the last minute, instead of falling back into behaviors that might not serve me, I can remember my commitment by bringing my vow into my awareness. Then I am reminded of how I want to act in my relationship with Dan. My divorce vow shines a light into my heart so that I can remember who I am in my highest expression, even in my lowest moments.

This is the divorce vow that I use today:

I, Debbie, take you, Dan, to be my partner in co-parenting a healthy, loving child. I promise to support you in having an exciting, nurturing relationship with our son. I am committed to being flexible with my schedule and open with my feelings, and to creating together an effortless and loving rhythm to join our two families with one heart.

I created my divorce vow by closing my eyes, connecting with my heart, and asking myself, *What would be the highest expression of an extraordinary relationship with Dan?* This divorce vow emerged and has become my guiding force. Now, whenever there are problems or upsets, I look to see whether my action or reaction is consistent with my commitment to honoring my divorce vow. If it's not, I look to see what I need to do to alter my behavior. I know that I can't lose if I stay true to my highest commitments to Dan, Beau, and myself.

We have to continually examine our actions to keep them consistent with our highest commitments. We need to be honest about what's important and what's not. Often we get wrapped up in the big stuff. The big career move, the new car, or the next relationship. But a true sense of self-worth arises out of the little things we do—choosing to say yes instead of no, to give in instead of to fight. Nothing can make us feel better than being able to tell our children that we're proud of our choices, having the self-esteem to look everyone in the eye, and feeling proud enough to pat ourselves on the back for the deeds we did today.

Now is when we must develop an intimate and close relationship with ourselves, taking the time to listen to our inner voices and acting in ways that bring out the best in ourselves. There is nothing more beautiful than a person who embraces his or her entire self. A person who feels complete and whole radiates confidence and exudes internal power.

This is a time when you need to move slowly, carefully nurturing yourself through each decision, examining each of your actions, knowing that the choices you make today are shaping your life for the future. Now is when you must give yourself permission to remember your dreams and make a decision to create the best life you can imagine. This is a sacred time when you can build a strong foundation that will hold and support you as you evolve into the person you want to be. Divorce is a transformational time, and you can choose to use it as the fuel for creating an extraordinary life.

The moment you have the life you've dreamed of you will thank God for your divorce experience, no matter how difficult the circumstances. You will naturally honor your ex-partner and support those around you in accepting your divorce. You will choose to keep your heart soft at times when you would have hardened it. Falling into the softness of your heart means slowing down, dropping your expectations, and looking and living in the moment. When we are quiet enough, we reconnect with our inner knowing that life is progressing as it should. We can then breathe in the scent of a new beginning and open up to the magical gifts that life brings.

Our soul's desire is to express itself completely and unabashedly. All we have to do is stay out of the narrow confines of our intellects and melt into the warm, loving presence of our forgiving hearts. We are divinely guided and programmed with all the information we need to arrive at the perfect destination. Henry David Thoreau said, "You must live in the present and launch yourself on every wave. Discover your eternity in each moment." If we choose to let go and enjoy the ride of our highest expression, we will be blessed with the privilege of coming face to face with our own magnificence.

The greatest lesson of my life was echoed in words by Albert Einstein: "There are only two ways to live your life. One is as though nothing is a miracle. The other is as though everything is a miracle." I support you in choosing a miracle.

HEALING ACTION STEPSE

1. Create a divorce vow that will inspire you to behave in ways consistent with the kind of person you want to be. Share your divorce vow with two people, and enlist the support of your friends and family to keep you true to this higher vision.

2. The following exercise is a visual reminder of the future that you want to call forth. Take a few minutes to meditate before beginning this exercise. Look through all your favorite magazines. Gather pictures that inspire you. Select ten to twenty images that represent things you love, places you would like to go, or activities you want to be doing. Find images and words that excite you. Try not to think too much as you make your selections; allow your unconscious to guide you. Then take a piece of cardboard or construction paper and put together a collage that calls forth an exciting future. Hang it in a place where you can see it daily.

3. Make a list of your daily behaviors and practices. Then make another list of what you believe would be the behaviors and practices of an extraordinary person. Compare your lists and decide what adjustments you'd be willing to make.

4. Take two risks every week for the next four weeks. Take a yoga class, go to a support group, get a makeover, purchase new clothes, or take a hike in the woods. Take risks that enhance your self-esteem, then write in your journal about how you felt after nurturing yourself.

ACKNOWLEDGMENTS

To the talented and wonderful Liz Perle, my editor-in-chief, for always asking for more and demanding the best out of me. Thank you for sharing all your wisdom and for giving so much to this project. I honor you.

To my brilliant and talented sister, Arielle Ford, whose dreams for me are always bigger than my own. Thank you for being there for me every day, for guiding me to bring forth my best. I do not have words to convey the depth of my love for you. Big kisses.

To my beloved brother-in-law, Brian Hilliard, for being "my people." Thank you for watching over me and for taking such good care of my sister.

To my very dear friend Danielle Dorman. Your wise eyes have been an incredible guide for me. Thank you for all the love, care, and support you have provided for me. Your contribution to this book has been a precious gift. I love you.

To my most devoted supporter, Rachel Levy. Thank you for the ways in which you contribute to my life and my work. You are a brilliant gem and your presence makes a huge difference.

To my beloved mother, Sheila Fuerst. Thank you for moving to be near us and for being the best mom and grandma in the whole world.

To my second father, Howard Fuerst. Your discipline and commitment to wholeness inspire me every day. Thank you for the huge contribution you make in my life.

To my precious father in heaven, Harvey Ford. I feel your presence every time I write, and I know you are up there rooting for me. I miss you.

To my ex-husband, Dan. Thank you for always choosing what's in the highest good for Beau and for continually supporting me in my career. You are an extraordinary human being and I deeply respect you.

To my sweet earth angel Alisha Schwartz. No words can express the gratitude I feel for the love and nurturing you provide for me. You are a bright star in my life and I love you.

To Sid Ayers for being here for me every single day and for taking care of all the many details of my life. You are a special woman and you make a huge difference.

To my brother Michael Ford (a.k.a. Mikie) for always being here for me and for reading my unedited words over and over again. Thank you for generously sharing your wisdom.

To Geeta Singh and the Talent Exchange. Thank you for taking such good care of me and helping to get the messages I carry out into the world. You are truly a saint.

To Dr. David Simon for being an extraordinary teacher, a great friend, and an inspiration to me always.

To Deepak Chopra for being a catalyst for my own transformation and for providing me with so many opportunities to grow as a teacher and a healer.

To Neale Donald Walsch. I treasure your support and friendship. Thank you for your coaching, your feedback, and for demanding that I finally write this book. I love you.

To Katherine Kellmeyer, Laura Clark, and The Ford Group— you are my PR angels. You'll never know how much I appreciate the work you do for me.

To my dear friend Stephen Samuels for guiding me in the right direction. Thank you for being brave enough to voice your opinions. You are very special to me.

To Henrietta Rosenberg for supporting my physical, emotional, and spiritual well-being while I wrote. You are an incredible healer and make a huge difference in my life.

To Cheryl Richardson for supporting me in the birth of *Spiritual*

Divorce. Thank you for your friendship and your expert coaching. I love you.

To Marianne Williamson for being a champion for *Spiritual Divorce* and for sharing all your wisdom with me.

To my friend Dennis Schmucker for being the first person to hold the vision for this book. Thank you for being an ally and confidante during my divorce.

To John McShane, my partner and cohort in our quest to transform the experience of divorce in our society. You are a champion of our times, and I am touched by the love you have for people suffering through the trauma of divorce.

To the irreplaceable and ever-reliable Cliff Edwards. Thank you for making sure my book didn't disappear into cyberspace. You are a master coach and a dear friend.

To my dear friend Justin Hilton. Your love for me has been a true gift. Thank you for all the support you provide for me.

To the loving staff of the Chopra Center for Well Being and especially to Nan Johnson. Your vision and dedication to all of us who are part of this magnificent family is the foundation for the work we are doing in the world.

To my brother Sorano Kelly and the Center for Excellence. Let's take a moment to fall still. . . . Good. You and the coaching program have touched my life.

To John Austin, Brent Becvar, Rama Berch, Beá (Bigman) Luba Bozanich, Rita Curtis, Sherri Davis, Jill Lawrence, Sarah McClean, Natalie Snyder, Jeremiah Sullivan, and all the members of my family. Thank you for the wisdom you have shared, the lessons you have taught me, and the love that you have given to me. Know that you have made a big difference in my life.

To Dr. Herb Goldberg for all of his profound wisdom and insight.

To Jeremiah Abrams for always being on the other end of the phone with me. Thank you for caring about the work that I do and for sharing your wisdom with me.

To Tim Donner and the amazingly talented staff of Sites of Mind for your creativity, vision, and dedication to making http://www.spiritualdivorce.com the most innovative and healing divorce site on the planet. Great work!

To David Hennessy, Rebecca Fox, Lisa Zuniga, and the amazingly supportive staff at HarperCollins who worked so hard on this book. Thank you very, very much.

To Lizzie Shaw, Debbie Myers, and the entire staff at www.mypotential.com for your commitment and support in bringing forth healing on the planet.

To all the people who shared your stories. Thank you for working so hard to transform your reality, for courageously turning your pain into wisdom and your sadness into joy. I admire you.

To all the people I have not mentioned by name. You are in my heart and I love you.

And a special thanks to my Grandma Ada, who always told me, "You can do it!"

To the Spirit that runs through me, that guides and protects me and that willingly gives me all the support and knowledge that I need, I am totally devoted to you.

To contact Debbie Ford
and for information on her workshops:

Debbie Ford
P.O. Box 8064
La Jolla, CA 92038
800-655-4016
www.debbieford.com